I Wrote This Book Because I Love You

Essays

Tim Kreider

Simon & Schuster Paperbacks
New York London Toronto Sydney New Delhi

Simon & Schuster Paperbacks
An Imprint of Simon & Schuster, Inc.
1230 Avenue of the Americas
New York, NY 10020

The following selections were previously published in the *New York Times*: "Oof" (as "I Know What You Think of Me"), "The Feast of Pain," "A Man and His Cat," "On Smushing" (as "On Smushing Bugs"), and "I Never Went to Iceland" (as "The Summer That Never Was").

First Simon & Schuster trade paperback edition February 2019

Interior design by Lewelin Polanco

Manufactured in the United States of America

10 9 8 7 6 5 4 3

Library of Congress Cataloging-in-Publication data is available.

ISBN 978-1-4767-3899-4
ISBN 978-1-4767-3901-4 (pbk)
ISBN 978-1-4767-3902-1 (ebook)

Praise for *I Wrote This Book Because I Love You*

"In a style reminiscent of Orwell, E. B. White, and David Sedaris, an affable hero gamely bumbles through adventures rich with moments of fleeting profundity and moral reckoning. . . . His depictions of the arc from ignorance to wisdom are reliably deft. . . . Kreider is a curious and compassionate observer and a fantastic wit—I laughed to tears more than once. . . . Pleasurable, well-wrought essays."

—*The New York Times Book Review*

"Tim Kreider's voice is never anything less than honest, smart, and hilarious; in *I Wrote This Book Because I Love You* he is even more mordant and empathetic than ever before. What a sad and beautiful book."

—Lauren Groff, author of *Fates and Furies*

"Tim Kreider's wonderfully frank, consistently funny essays reminded me at a time of spectacular doubt that there might still be a few men in America who are both weird and wise, equally friendly to cats and ex-girlfriends, and refreshingly willing to admit to flaws that come entirely free of vindictiveness and cruelty. In an age of widespread buffoonery, it's a pleasure and a relief to have Kreider restore a little faith."

—Joshua Ferris, author of *The Dinner Party and Other Stories*

"Not only smart, but admission-against-interest honest—a winning combination, and rare."

—Lionel Shriver

"Tim Kreider is one of my favorite living writers, no exaggeration. . . . His wisdom is counterintuitive and therefore all the wiser; his humor is dark in ways that let light in where it's needed most. This isn't a book about one man's relationship to women as much as it's a chart of the collision course of human need in all its wrenching, perverse, gorgeous, hilarious forms. It's his best stuff yet."

—Meghan Daum, author of *The Unspeakable: And Other Subjects of Discussion*

"Kreider . . . writes like a smart, funny friend; his essays feel like late-night conversations that you don't want to end."

—*The Seattle Times*

"A talented writer . . . [Tim Kreider's] essays are beautifully written, with just enough humor to balance his spikiness, and will please lovers of fine writing."

—*Booklist*

"Kreider isn't solely a humorist; he's also part philosopher, part psychologist, part poet. Paired with his depth of insight into the human condition and startlingly sharp observations, this intimate collection is as hilarious as it is poignant, as it explores what it means to love and be loved—even if it's love shared with your 19-year-old cat."

—*Baltimore* magazine

"The theme running through this book's dozen essays is Kreider's relationships with women, platonic and romantic, and he recounts them with wonderfully self-deprecating wit and considerable insight."

—*Tampa Bay Times*

"Kreider is . . . an inimitable American essayist. He reliably, intelligently, wittily states the hesitated-over, the unspoken, the perhaps, the after-last-call-drunken-theory-of-the-universe that actually might have been brilliant. His ideas are sometimes risky or incomplete, but I've almost never encountered them anywhere else; in style, he sits on the shelf between the quick humor of Dave Barry and the gentle, erudite persuasion of Virginia Woolf. When reading Tim Kreider, I feel as if he's stated what's already in my mind."

—*Another Chicago Magazine*

"Much of the collection's strength comes from wry ruminations on his non-romantic relationships. . . . Kreider's observations cut deep, sharply delivered in the midst of what he might sometimes call 'mush.' It's no surprise that David Foster Wallace declared, 'Kreider rules,' or that Kreider counts Richard Russo and Judd Apatow as fans. His precision and candor coexist like a just-sharpened razor slicing into soft fruit, sweet, lovely, messy, and sustaining."

—Shelf Awareness

"Come for the arresting cover, stay for the author's trenchant ruminations on his relationships with women. . . . Like all the best essayists, Kreider finds words for the ineffable . . . he'll open your eyes to the many varieties of love."

—*People*

"Kreider . . . deploys an extremely self-deprecating tone, which comes across as appealing and humorous and, sometimes, laugh-out-loud funny. . . . The pieces are piercingly, painfully reflective. . . . An artful example of how the deeply personal can also be the broadly general."

—*Kirkus Reviews*

"Kreider . . . returns with another incisive and cutting collection of essays, this time loosely focused on the women in his life. . . . This collection is noteworthy not so much for the insights into dating or women, but rather for Kreider's humane outlook coupled with his often-wry sense of humor. . . . [His] clever hand and philosophic—rather than solipsistic—viewpoint place him in a different realm."

—*Publishers Weekly*

Also by Tim Kreider

We Learn Nothing

Twilight of the Assholes

Why Do They Kill Me?

The Pain: When Will It End?

For my sisters—adoptive, half, and chosen

One of the greatest gifts you can give anybody is the gift of your honest self.

—Fred ("Mister") Rogers

Whatever is done out of love always occurs beyond good and evil.

—Friedrich Nietzsche, *Beyond Good and Evil*

DRAMATIS PERSONÆ

TIM, *our Narrator.*
ANNIE, *an Invalid.*
ZACH, *her scorned Betrothed.*
LOU, *a Clown.*
ZOEY, *a Harlot.*
HAROLD, *a Rascal.*
MISHKA, *a Rogue.*
LAUREN, *an Artist.*
LARS, *her Husband.*
GEORGE, *a Fool.*
KATI JO, *a Libertine.*
LUCY, *Friend and Counselor.*

T.J., *a Polyamorist.*
KEVIN, *a faithless Husband.*
THE QUETZAL, *a Cat.*
MARGOT, *a Journalist.*
SILVIA BELL, *a learnèd Doctor.*
ROSALIND, *a Youth.*
GINA, *an Actress.*
DIANA, *a Clergywoman.*
FRIEDRICH, *a Philosopher.*

Circus Troupe, with Animals, and assorted Students and Bohemians.

SCENE—In AMERICA, with an Excursion to MEXICO.

Contents

* Note to Mom: do not read.

A Note on Veracity

Although I am scrupulous about sticking to the truth to the best of my recall, and am bad at making things up, this isn't to say that other people featured as characters in these essays wouldn't have different, sometimes conflicting recollections. But almost all of them have read the essays in which they appear and more or less graciously given their approval.

I have in a few cases elided or altered details in order to disguise people's identities. And I've changed everybody's names, except for those of public figures like Nietzsche and George.

As always, I had to keep all the best stuff out.

Death-Defying Acts

"Say, I think if we got married you could ride the circus train to Mexico with me for free," Annie wrote in a P.S. to a postcard to me in 1998. "Think about it." The card's front bore a Richard Avedon portrait of William S. Burroughs, whose shriveled visage will always be associated in my memory with my first proposal of marriage.

Annie had run off to join the circus after breaking up with her last boyfriend, who was, among other things, a unicyclist and a juggler. I'd driven the getaway car when she'd left all of his belongings and everything he'd ever given her on his porch with a melodramatically worded note placed atop the pile. She'd answered a cryptic classified ad for a teaching position in the *Miami Herald*, gone in for an interview, and unexpectedly found herself working for the famous Ringling Bros. and Barnum & Bailey Circus, living on a train with roustabouts, clowns, and hippopotami. She was actually employed by the same agency that provides teachers to child actors on movie sets; by law, all U.S. children have to have 180 days of schooling a year, whether they're starring in a *Spy Kids* sequel or being publicly flung from one parent to another fifty feet above the ground, and Annie's job was to ensure that the children of aerialists got the same education as their earthbound peers. She had complained to me that education wasn't especially valued in the circus; the general attitude was: *What do you need with some diploma? You'll always have the trapeze.* But she loved her life on board the train, riding the rails from city to city, setting up her portable one-room classroom in the dingy innards of downtown arenas. I'd visited her at Baltimore's civic center when the circus had come to town, where, to get to her classroom, I'd had to sidle between tigers sacked out in their cages like half-ton house cats. It provided her ideal living situation, she explained: "Constant change within a framework of structure." Annie had always liked road trips, sleeper cars, hotels and room service; her childhood heroine had been Eloise, the little girl who lived in the Plaza.

I took her proposal less seriously than you might think, and not only because it came in a P.S. I knew a number of people who had believed themselves, at various times, to be engaged to Annie. She was famously once engaged to two men at the same time: our friend Zach, who had a history of moving across the country to begin his new life with Annie only to find himself dumped on arrival, and Poor, Poor Ted, a very sad avant-garde composer. Annie downplays that whole episode as a miscommunication or slight overlap in timing. Zach is philosophical about it now: "Annie was more excitable in those days," he sighs. She and I had nearly gotten married once, too, in the Mall of America's wedding chapel, but this was more in the nature of a caper, and in any case we were foiled by the state's buzzkill twenty-four-hour waiting period.

Annie and I knew each other and ourselves too well to delude ourselves that we would do anything other than drive each other insane if we were ever to attempt to date. We were like each other's evil twins: we were both adopted, both had mitral valve prolapse, our younger sisters were both named Laurie, and our fathers had both died of cancer when we were in college. Our relationship was partly predicated on unrepentant selfishness; the tacit shtick between us was that neither of us really cared about anyone but ourselves, so around each other we could quit faking and relax. I'd once watched with interest as a New York City con artist had tried to exploit Annie's sympathy and guilt; it was as though he were dealing three-card monte for the blind. The only thing that reliably made her weep was the poignant theme from the old *Incredible Hulk* TV show.

I'd also been Annie's traveling companion before, and knew to be wary of hidden agendas. On a cross-country trip a few years earlier—the same one that began with our leaving the pile of possessions on her ex's doorstep—we'd detoured a whole day's drive up into the Idaho panhandle before she revealed, over beers, that we were there to perpetrate another caper: I was to photograph her gloating in front of her ex's summer cabin, where he had never once taken her, which photo she would then send to him.

So I was unsurprised to learn that the real reason she wanted me to travel to Mexico, and to marry her, was for protection. She'd been hearing about how dangerous Mexico City was and been told that, as a single woman, she could expect to be ceaselessly harassed, so she thought she might be safer with a husband along to escort her. I was not anyone's first choice for a bodyguard—in fact, I had a history of being assaulted abroad*—but I was well known to be unemployed and always game for a caper.

Annie was either more acutely conscious of her mortality or less able to deal with it than anyone else I've ever known; she feared it in the same visceral way that other people are terrified of spiders or heights. One night in college, when she was having one of her panic attacks about death, she flipped frantically through the TV

* See the essay "Reprieve" in my book *We Learn Nothing*, if you're really interested.

channels trying to find something to distract her, and she happened across a Ginger Rogers/Fred Astaire movie called *Carefree*. Annie was entranced. The film did exactly as advertised: made her forget herself for a couple of hours in a lighthearted dream of elegance and grace. Human beings never were more lovely, more perfect in motion. Annie is not a halfway kind of girl, and for the next several years she became obsessed with Ginger Rogers: she talked incessantly about Ginger Rogers, amassed as complete a collection of Ginger Rogers movies as could be found on VHS, and made a pilgrimage to Ginger Rogers's ranch in Oregon, which was not open to the public. (A very polite personal assistant gave her a tour of the grounds and an autographed photo before shooing her off.) Ginger Rogerism was a perfectly serviceable religion: Annie did not try to convert unbelievers or burn heretics alive; she'd found solace in a harmless fantasy of athletic perfection and deathless beauty, in frivolous spectacle.

But in this case Annie wasn't (just) being paranoid; the Mexican economy had collapsed in 1994, and over the next three years crime in Mexico City increased by nearly 60 percent: by 1997 there were an average of three murders, ninety-four assaults on pedestrians, seventy-eight assaults on drivers, and twenty-five home invasions per day. For a while there was no nightlife in the city; bars, restaurants, theaters, and clubs all shut down at dusk because no one would venture out after dark. In 1998, when Annie invited me to go, the U.S. State Department reported that violence "had reached critical levels."

The official State Department warnings on Mexico, which took some time to print out, cited recent incidents of Americans being murdered, kidnapped, raped in taxis, drugged in bars, and accidentally slammed into the sides of hotels while parasailing. They made it sound like open season on gringos down there. Annie told me everyone at the circus had been studying this same printout. I figured people who walked on the high wire and got into cages with wild animals nightly probably had more accurate risk-assessment skills than civilians, so I asked her: "So, do people at the circus seem worried, or . . . ?"

"Everyone's petrified."

Although I didn't suffer from the same sort of acute thanatophobia as Annie, I'd always been uncomfortably conscious of what Francis Bacon* called "the potential disaster that stalks us every day," even before I got stabbed in Crete. The morbid imagination we shared had always been another bond between us. (I'd once reduced her to weeping with glee by delivering a mock funeral oration for her: "But, in the end, it wasn't her deviousness, or even her perversity that made her so ornery; it was the *malice* of the woman.") And Mexico offered no shortage of material for the morbid imagination. The "Dangers and Annoyances" section of the guidebook I consulted ran to several pages, covering annoyances from Cholera to Volcanic Activity. I was advised by friends that I would inevitably contract dysentery from the food, and told "your mucus will turn black" from the air pollution, the worst in the hemisphere. So I was, understandably, a little skittish.

Nevertheless my policy has always been, whenever someone proposes I marry them and ride the circus train with them to Mexico City, to say: Yes. And Annie's postcard had found me convalescing on my sofa in the aftermath of a romantic imbroglio known to history as "Armageddon '97," so I was in need of a distraction. An adventure. Something to get a man up off his couch and moving again. It was one of those situations in which you get to pretend you're coming to someone's rescue when secretly they're coming to yours.

Although I was not required to legally marry Annie, I would at least have to pose as her husband, since only spouses were allowed to ride the train, not boyfriends or other freeloaders. The

* The painter, not the philosopher.

plan was that I would meet the circus train in Roanoke, Virginia, and we would ride it together for three days down to the Mexican border. The train no longer traveled all the way to Mexico City, because back when it did they'd had to erect a fence around it and post guards to protect it against thieves. Now everyone disembarked in San Antonio and flew the rest of the way down, while a shorter section of the train carrying the animals and equipment continued on to Mexico City. Annie and I, in deference to her flying phobia—which she always emphasized was not a fear of heights or falling or incineration but of "loss of *control*"—would be taking the bus, a twenty-hour journey.

In Roanoke, I found Annie in road-trip mode, her long red hair braided into two Pippi Longstocking pigtails, wearing denim overalls over a striped shirt, which left small triangles of pale midriff exposed on either side that were very hard not to poke. One of the first things she did after I arrived was to make me feel a lump on her back. She had mentioned this lump several times on the phone. She was certain it was a tumor. Annie had suffered from a case of hypochondria for years, which had been triumphantly vindicated the year before when she'd been diagnosed with lupus, the disease that killed Flannery O'Connor. Back in O'Connor's day it was generally assumed that if you had lupus you were going to die young. This was no longer necessarily true by the 1990s, but it was still incurable, and had "a significant morbidity rate." Survival rates decreased steadily over time, so that although Annie was 90 percent likely to be alive five years from now, in 2003, she was less than 70 percent likely to make it to the year 2018. Her doctor had strongly recommended that Annie stop researching her illness on Internet message boards.

You'd think that controlling a chronic disease would provide an outlet for her hypochondria and obsessive tendencies, but by now Annie wasn't making a big deal of the lupus anymore. She had to take antimalarials and aspirin for inflammation after eating, and periodically had blood drawn to monitor her antibody levels. The condition was also a convenient excuse to avoid the sun and the outdoors, both of which Annie had always hated. Whenever anyone, learning about her diagnosis, asked, "Is there anything I can do for you?" she always answered: "You could give me fifty dollars." (My ex-girlfriend Margot had sent her a check along with a note: *Dear Annie, I am very sorry you have lupus. Here are fifty dollars for you.*) She still found the energy to worry about other, unrelated anomalies, such as the suspect lump.

She pulled up the back of her shirt, felt around for it with her arm twisted up between her shoulder blades, and pressed my fingers into it. The lump was about the size of a Junior Mint, and jiggled slightly under pressure. My own diagnosis was that it was one of those weird things that just appears for no reason and would probably go away on its own. Her doctor had told her it was "adipose tissue," which I knew very well meant it was a fat lump. Annie preferred to refer to it as adipose tissue and continued to monitor it closely, regarding it as premalignant at best.

My first night on board, Annie took me on a tour of the train. The hallways weren't quite wide enough for two people to pass, so if you saw someone coming, you'd politely race to step aside in the bathroom alcove in the center of the car. Some of the doors were personalized with signs or stickers ("Still Pissed at Yoko") or had homey little welcome mats laid out front. Each car had its own distinct smell, like each of your childhood friends' houses, ranging from antiseptic to uric to sweet-and-sour pork. Annie told me this was the longest privately owned train in the world, over a mile from engine to caboose, with thirty-two coaches, not counting flatcars and animal cars. Highlights of our tour would include the Clown Car, the Ghetto Car, and the Pie Car.

"Did you say 'the Ghetto Car'?" I asked.

"You'll see," she told me.

The circus train constituted a stark microcosmic class hierarchy, wherein space = status. The stars of the show, the chief clown and the tiger tamer, each had an entire car for their families; the rank-and-file clowns got rooms the size of wardrobes, about three by six feet. Annie's room was respectably spacious, though still tiny by normal standards. What Annie liked best about it was that she didn't have to get out of bed to get anything; the minifridge, hot plate, sink, closet, tape player, VCR, and TV remote were all within reach, any loose items secured with bungee cords. (She warned me that the train would jolt violently at night.) It was an ideal room for an aspiring invalid.

Because their rooms were so cramped, the clowns tended to leave their doors open and congregate in the hall; they called it a "dorm on wheels." When we passed through the Clown Car, the clowns were all hanging out in the kitchen, making dinner and listening to a Michael Jackson tape. They were essentially theater kids—attention-getters and cutups—so someone was always singing, juggling, playing outdoor sports indoors, or whanging someone else over the head with a cookie sheet. There was a mosaic of photos on the wall in which, on a cursory inspection, I found two pictures of naked people in clown makeup. Only the faces were painted.

Annie paused to brief me outside the door marked GENERATOR CAR, in which it would be too loud for us to talk. "The Ghetto Car is on the other side of this car," she said. "We'll have to blow through pretty fast so it doesn't look like we're there to gawk. Also," she admitted, "it kinda scares me in there." Then she opened the door to a clattering din and we clamped our hands over our ears and ran. When I had to unclamp one hand to open the door at the other end of the car, the noise physically hurt. As we walked nonchalantly but quickly through the Ghetto Car, I saw that people in there didn't even get rooms, just sleeping berths with curtains, like sailors' hammocks belowdecks. Once we were through, Annie explained that the circus would pick up itinerant workers—what civilians would call the homeless—keep them aboard for as long as they needed the extra hands, and then kick them off wherever they happened to be when they didn't require them anymore. "They're basically hobos," she said.

Pie car is circus slang for the dining car. There is no pie there. It smelled like greasy frying breakfast, brewing coffee, and cigarette smoke. The curtains were patterned with a row of pigs' butts lined up at a trough. A TV was showing one of the two movies continuously running on the train's closed-circuit system. Eavesdropping in the Pie Car was one of the only ways I had of getting any inside information about life in the circus. Because they've long been regarded as vagrants and pariahs, circus folk are an insular society; you're either with the circus or you're not. And being "with" the circus means for life; careers are hereditary, acts dynastic. A lot of performers come from old circus families in eastern Europe. Annie, who'd been here the better part of a year, was still viewed as a transient and an outsider. But in the Pie Car I could eat a Belly Buster (cheeseburger with bacon and a fried egg on top) and listen in on the roustabouts bitching about the boredom, the overtime, and the animal rights workers who demonstrated at every arena ("Yeah, like they're not wearing leather shoes"). I got to hear the cotton candy man say: "When I finish makin' that candy, man, I'm *done*."

"Enough of this excitement," one guy announced on my first morning, putting out a cigarette in his plate. "Time for beer."

"You'll see plenty of drinking here," Annie was warned when she joined the circus. "All times of day." Annie and I liked to drink beers in the vestibule between her car and the next, which had a Dutch door we could open to the air. We'd sit dangling our legs over the side and occasionally poke our heads out into the wind and noise. If you stuck your hand out there when a tree branch was whipping past, the leaves would smack your palm hard enough to sting for minutes. Lights flashed and clanging bells Dopplered by as we passed through intersections. As the train traveled farther south, the metal swing sets, piles of tires, and misty hills of

Appalachia gave way to groves of bamboo and honeysuckle, fields plowed in undulating green and yellow lines like contour maps. We saw a woman standing in her lawn in her housedress, a pit filled with cattle bones, a repairman bent over exposing what looked like two feet of ass crack. Once, when we had stopped for a minute, I leapt down off the train and quick grabbed us some honeysuckle to taste while Annie went "*Aaiiieeeee*" and flapped her hands in delighted alarm.

As we sat drinking beers and watching the passing countryside, we'd spin elaborate worst-case scenarios: I would survive Mexico City but ironically die in a plane crash on the way home; Annie would avoid flying but be ironically killed in a bus wreck; my plane would crash ironically into her bus. We imagined both of us peering out of the train door and getting our heads neatly skwapped off by a passing train or telephone pole and our lifeless torsos, now open fire hydrants of blood, toppling back into the vestibule. Annie has very loose, jiggly kneecaps that were fun to slither around under her skin while we talked.

"You know the trainmaster will throw you off the train if he catches you doing that," someone passing through the vestibule told us. He meant dangling our legs out of the train. Annie told me he probably wasn't exaggerating: the circus's management philosophy was very nineteenth-century. The basic contract was: *You don't like it, get off the train.* So we stood instead, leaning over the closed lower door to look outside. When we were on a bend in the track, the wheels screeching against the rails, you could see nothing but train curving away in either direction, people leaning out the windows and doors to wave and give each other the finger. For the first time I could appreciate the train's true length; it was like being inside the Empire State Building laid on its side. Big red circus letters painted on the sides of the cars advertised who we were. No one can resist waving to the circus train; one group even waved to us from a cemetery. We had no choice but to wave back, conscripted into service as ambassadors of goodwill. Sometimes Annie wore a red clown nose while waving. At one crossing, a man sitting in the cab of his pickup waiting for the train to pass got to see Annie, wearing the nose, flash her breasts at him. I caught a glimpse of his face bursting into laughter before he was whisked into the past.

We were hanging out in the vestibule when one of the concessionaires approached us and mumbled, "Now, I don't mean nuthin' funny"—a sure sign of impending funniness—"but I never knew the teacher was married. Some of the things I said . . . I shouldn'a said them." It seemed he was trying to apologize for having flirted with Annie, apparently so clumsily she'd failed to notice. She told him it was fine, but she didn't like knowing that people were talking about us. She was still seething over having been teased in print for being standoffish by "Big Bertha," the circus newsletter's anonymous gossip columnist. Even more than most workplaces, the circus was a hotbed of gossip—after all, everyone not only worked together but lived together. It was effectively a small town. One of the dancers later asked me whether Annie and I were really married, boyfriend-girlfriend, just friends, or what.

"Just friends," I answered, after a telltale hesitation.

"Liar," she said.

I mean it's true we were having sex. But this was more in the spirit of two people who happen to have a common enthusiasm for an extremely fun activity, the same way two guys who both enjoy drinking or chess might say, "It's five o'clock somewhere" or "How about a quick game?" Once, when we were hanging out in the vestibule, the train hit an especially rough stretch of track, and one of us idly wondered what it would be like to try to have sex during this severe rhythmic jouncing. We exchanged a look. An instant later we had vamoosed, leaving a cartoon Annie-and-me-shaped puff of dust where we'd been standing.

After we disembarked in San Antonio, Annie made it a mission to buy wedding rings before crossing the border as a prophylactic against harassment. We got a pair of fake gold bands from a street vendor for five bucks apiece. It was funny: even though I never notice whether anyone else is wearing a wedding ring, I immediately felt as if mine were radiating my bogus marital status to everyone in sight. It seemed as if we ought to have some sort of ceremony. As we put them on, I said to Annie: "Now we are man and wife."

"Man," she snickered.

On the eve of our departure for Mexico we went to see a movie about an asteroid destroying all life on Earth and wept at the scene of the doomed astronauts saying farewell to their loved ones back home. Annie called her mother that night. The next day, at the bus station, we agonized over whether to take the 1:30 or the 2:30 to Mexico City, since there was no way of knowing in advance which of them was destined to crash, decapitating all on board. I got all calm and fatalistic and told Annie it was out of our hands—we'd just have to choose blindly.

At the border, Annie took longer than everyone else going through the customhouse because she had to obtain a work visa. I was on the bus waiting for her when the driver stood up and asked us all something in Spanish. I realized he was trying to confirm that everyone was back on board, and I stood up and used my first public Spanish: "No!" (I know it's the same word as in English, but I yelled it with a Spanish accent.) Everyone turned to look at me. "*Mi esposa*," I explained, gesturing helplessly toward the customs building. Everyone smiled, understanding. It was the only word I could think of.

The economic escarpment at the border was dramatic: the asphalt and neon of backstreet America turned abruptly to dirt roads, hand-lettered signs, kids piled into the backs of pickup trucks, and livestock just standing in the middle of the street. For a couple of hundred miles we saw nothing but prickly pear and Joshua trees, with an occasional line of jagged peaks on the horizon. We used our time on the bus to attempt to hastily learn Spanish and jot down some wills. Looking for safety instructions, I stuck my hand in the pocket on the back of the seat in front of me, into what proved to be a gooey orange burrito stuffed with hair. It seemed an ill omen.

Annie had been somewhat reassured of our odds after phoning her mother, who'd told her that all her old-lady friends had been going to Mexico City for years and none of them had ever been kidnapped or killed. The State Department's been issuing those same warnings for twenty years, she said.

"Of course, my mom dismissed my lupus symptoms for a year before I was diagnosed," said Annie. "You know what she said to me when I told her I had it? 'Well, dear, everybody's got to have something.'"

"Danger is almost always less than you imagine it to be," our hotel's guidebook assured us.

The hotel where most of the circus workers were being put up was on a heavy-flow eight-lane street across from a Wal-Mart. On the afternoon we arrived there was a windstorm that blotted out the view with dense gusts of dust and grit and garbage, airborne because the city had been completely denuded of grass. It was like the weather on Mars. I asked one of the clowns who was originally from Mexico City whether the sky was ever blue here.

"Yes," he said.

"Really?"

"I don't know," he admitted.

The hotel guidebook also mentioned, as a point of local color, that the nearby Hill of the Star had in pre-Columbian times been the site of the New Fire ceremony, in which, once every fifty-two years, a sacrificial victim's heart would be carved out and a fire lit in his chest cavity. It was sort of like Groundhog Day: if the fire continued to burn, runners would light torches from it and take them to temples throughout the empire to let people know that the world would continue to exist. The book did not say what happened if the fire went out.*

Over dinner in the hotel restaurant that night, I reassured Annie that I wouldn't blame her, in my last moments, if I were to be killed here.

"No," she said, "I'd blame myself."

"I appreciate that," I said, "but I wouldn't want you to feel bad about it for the rest of your life."

"How long?"

"Well, you should always feel a *little* bad about it, but don't let it ruin your life."

"I'll never forgive myself," she said solemnly. I noticed she was talking about it in the future tense now instead of the good old conditional.

"The main thing to remember," I said, "is that I liked you a lot and you made the last year of my life much better."

"Aw," said Annie, sounding genuinely touched for once. "You really sound like you're going to die."

This sort of paranoia was rampant throughout the circus. In the hotel lobby I'd noticed one of the musicians reading a book titled *The Most Dangerous Places in the World*. On the shuttle bus a dancer said, "I thought *Baltimore* was scary." Annie overheard the tiger tamer talking to his wife long-distance on a pay phone, complaining about being afraid of the food, eating nothing but steak day after day. By way of a sign-off he said, "I'll try not to die."

On our first full day in Mexico City, the entire circus was assembled in the arena for a briefing by a representative of the American

---

* Further research has determined that what would happen was that skeleton women with eyes and teeth all over their bodies would descend from the stars and kill everyone in the world with knives and devour their flesh.

embassy. He wearily reiterated the State Department warnings we'd all by now memorized: the spiked drinks, the ATM robberies, the deathtrap taxis. A worst-case scenario, he said, would involve being kidnapped for anywhere from twelve to seventy-two hours, driven around the city, and forced to withdraw money from ATMs at gunpoint. "Crime in Mexico City is virtually a risk-free proposition," he told us, reciting it like a well-worn phrase. Often, he was sorry to say, the police themselves were the perpetrators. I found I was more disturbed by the thought of my death going unavenged than by the thought of being murdered. In conclusion he said, "I wish you the best of luck."

Most of the performers kept themselves insulated from the sprawling, impoverished metropolis around them, moving between their hotels and the arena in shuttle buses. Tourists were targeted in particular because they were perceived as wealthy, which, relative to most people in Mexico City, we were: to beggars and street thieves, even the roustabouts must've looked like Princess Diana. The first day Annie and I ventured into a city market, we had to run a gauntlet of merchants and vendors stepping into our path, each grinning and saying, "Something more, señor? Something more, señor?" A tiny woman pulled at Annie's sleeve, begging for money to buy a tortilla with a hand to her stomach, her mouth open and twisted with weeping. A shoeshine boy chased me down the street, shining one of my shoes against my will while I politely tried to flee.

Five centuries ago this was one of the most beautiful cities on earth: an island of pyramidal temples and palaces, botanical gardens, aquariums, and canals, at the center of a vast shallow lake that mirrored the sky, linked to the mainland by long causeways and aqueducts. All razed by the armies of Cortés. Annie and I toured the cathedral built atop the ruins of the Aztec temple, where we stood before the Altar of Forgiveness—something of a euphemism, it emerged—where heretics were brought to repent before being absolved and then set on fire. We also checked out the Palace of the

Inquisition, which now houses a medical museum, where a cadaver lay under a glass case like a flayed Sleeping Beauty, arteries dyed with bright pink gunk, stomach deflated, a flap of skin discreetly folded over the genitals, a few black curls of hair glistening underneath.

"Looks like chicken," Annie confirmed. She was right: the exposed fat—the adipose tissue—looked like a half-eaten drumstick left in the fridge to get cold and glutinous overnight. There was also a disembodied head displayed in a glass cube, half of which had been dissected, with little portholes cut into the skull through which you could view the brain. The other half of the face, left intact, looked like a guy you might see across from you on the bus. He did not look happy. Back at the hotel room I admitted that the cadavers had freaked me out.

"I detached myself from it," said Annie. "I only freaked out a little when I imagined having to eat it." I just looked at her. "Like in *Alive*," she clarified. Annie loved survival stories in which people have to resort to cannibalism.

After our first day out in Mexico City our lips tasted grimy, and we both had acrid postnasal drip. We showered and brushed our teeth and ordered a bucket of Coronas on ice from room service. (This would become our nightly ritual: almost twenty years later I still remember the phrase *un balde con hielo*.) That night, while we were drinking beers watching cable, Annie told me: "This morning I saw what you would look like when you're old. Kind of gray and jowly."

"Give me a break," I started. "I hadn't shaved yet, I wasn't—"

"No, no, it was good," she said. "It made me believe for the first time that maybe you would live."

The sights of Mexico City have gotten jumbled together in my memory with scenes backstage at the circus, like the contents of a suitcase disheveled in transit: police standing around in Kevlar vests idly holding automatic weapons, acrobats muscled like superheroes painted solid gold, teenage boys reading porn comics next to old ladies on the bus, a wardrobe pit crew quickly repairing a rip in a dancer's costume, bullet holes in the concrete over Trotsky's bed, ancient basalt blood basins, someone hosing out the hippo's open mouth, a dozen little chickens on a spit, midgets pushing a baby carriage, a begging child shaking a single maraca in a monotonous, unmusical rhythm, her face blank with rage. Somewhere in the arena an elephant trumpeted, and for an instant everyone froze.

As we watched the circus rehearse from high up in the arena's stands, Annie provided indispensable dishy backstage commentary: "Remember I told you how the one unicycle basketball team captain stabbed the other last year?" she'd say. "That's the one who got stabbed. There's the forty-year-old woman my eighteen-year-old student is marrying—second from the left. They all think it's just to get into the family act. Oh, and that's the guy who had the little, uh, domestic violence problem I told you about." During the star clown's act, he would force volunteers from the audience to wear tutus and perform a ballet routine. One elegant matron delighted the crowd by raising an outstretched leg to the barre with effortless aplomb. The clown gave her a *Well, well, well* look, hands on his hips. Annie told me she was a ringer—actually the clown's own mother, and a dancer with the circus from way back. Annie even knew the dirt on all the animals. She was caustic on the subject of animals who'd died; during the "First Day at School" skit, when the trainer called attendance and the baby elephants dutifully raised their trunks, Annie hissed, "Where's *Kenny*? Is Kenny out sick today?" As I watched a troupe of baboons in brightly colored diapers doing flips on the hippo's back, she leaned over and whispered, "Those monkeys have hideous, hideous asses."

After Annie started teaching, I spent a lot of my days with her best friend in the circus, Lou. Lou had actually attended the circus's famous Clown College, which he described as the greatest experience of his life: ten weeks of classes in pie throwing, water spitting, how to run in long floppy shoes. His instructor sounded like some sort of clown *rōshi*; he was heavily into what Lou calls "the heart of clowning," not just routines and technique. "If you're gonna be a clown," he'd tell his students, "you've gotta have a heart as big as Alaska! Clowning is snow on Christmas morning! It's an all-day sucker!" He and I visited the Basilica of Our Lady of Guadalupe together, where we rode a little conveyor belt past the miraculous image of the Virgin. Lou, a believer, admitted he had hoped it would look less like a painting.

Lou's secret ambition was to resurrect the Globe of Death, a spherical cage in which two motorcyclists would ride around and around, their orbits gradually spiraling sideways and then upside down, the two of them zooming around the sphere's meridians in perfect synchronization, all somehow without crashing into each other. I remembered it well from my own childhood trips to the circus. The old Globe was still in storage somewhere, like Excalibur in its stone, waiting for someone worthy to summon forth the balls to get in there again. I couldn't understand how you'd even practice this act without getting killed. Lou seemed confident that you'd just have to aim the bike straight ahead, get it up to speed, and let centrifugal force take care of the rest. He figured each rider would get the timing down independently, and then you'd go in there together and sort of work things out between the two of you. Annie told me Lou had never ridden a motorcycle.

Annie was jealous that I got to spend my days going on field trips with her friend while she was stuck in the classroom all day.

"Lou is coming between us, Annie," I told her. "Lou must die."

Her eyes lit up with an evil hope. "*He* is the one who will die in Mexico City!" she said.

"It's the only way we can save ourselves."

"Sacrifice!" she cried gleefully.

"Sacrifice! Sacrifice!" we both began chanting, bouncing up and down on the bed. "Lou must die! *Lou must die!*"

It was wrong of us to offer Lou as a sacrifice. Lou was a good guy. It was also probably foolhardy of us to invoke the old local gods in jest. I'd seen the goddess of death, Coatlicue, at the National Museum of Anthropology: wearing a tasteful necklace of human hands and hearts with a skull pendant and a mid-length skirt made of snakes, snakes also spurting from the decapitated stump of her neck (an Aztec artistic convention for blood), two of which were curled face-to-face to resemble a single grinning, fanged, and fork-tongued serpent, she was, to all appearances, not one to be summoned on a false alarm. And the circus was no place to risk jinxing anyone: there had recently been several serious injuries on the show. I'd seen a girl who had to walk around with both arms in casts propped up with sticks, raised over her head in what looked like triumph at all times. A performer in the other unit of the circus had been badly burned during a fire act. ("How's that guy doing?" I asked Annie. "Not good," she said.) And last month a woman working without a net had fallen forty feet from a trapeze at the D.C. Armory. This wasn't supposed to be possible, but somehow the cable attached to her harness had broken. She'd landed on her face. She was still on crutches, and one of her eyes was completely bloodshot. Lou had griped about the low attendance at shows in Mexico City; performers were up there, their lungs laboring in the filthy high-altitude air, risking their lives every night, for what—a couple of hundred spectators?

The circus doesn't have a doctor, Annie told me, or even EMTs; if someone gets hurt, they just call 911 and wait, like the rest of us. But there is a performance protocol in the event of an accident: there's one piece of music the orchestra plays when the trapeze artists make the triple somersault, and another to play if they don't. If there's a fall, the band whips up a jaunty, up-tempo nothin'-to-see-here number and the entire complement of clowns charges out in full force, deploying maximum antics to distract the audience. "'The show must go on,'" Annie said grimly.

After almost a month in Mexico City, my nerves had begun to go. It seemed as if not one second passed without the sound of a car horn playing "La Cucaracha," "Dixie," or the theme from *The*

Godfather. Annie told me I made this same observation every day. "Just tune it out, man," she snapped. The cry of the Chiclet hawkers on the metro, ending with the sustained moan "*Pesoooooooooooo*," started to sound inhuman and droning as a car alarm. The air always smelled like exhaust fumes and piss. I'd get winded after going up one flight of stairs. Phase one of the city's pollution control plan had been in effect for the last five days, a new record, and power plants had reduced their output to 60 percent, so that the hotel's lights kept flickering. The Palacio, the arena where the circus performed, was usually a dully gleaming bronze button on the horizon, but now it was barely visible through the dirty brown haze. It wasn't until two weeks into our stay that I'd discovered our room had a view of the mountains. I finally got the inevitable diarrhea after eating *pancita*, a soup made with tripe. Annie had watched in horror as I ate it, begging me to stop. ABUNDA MATERIAL FECAL EN COMIDA DE CALLEJERA, a recent headline had read. Annie translated *comida de callejera* as "street food." I didn't need help with the rest.

YANQI MATADO—another tabloid headline, accompanied by a photo of a feckless American goofball like myself. *Matado* turned out to mean not just *killed* but to connote something more like *slaughtered*. On the metro, I interrupted Annie in the middle of an extended daydream about being held up at gunpoint and having to explain to her assailant, in broken Spanish, why she had no valuables on her person. She had already worked out in her head rough phrases for "At pyramids yesterday, so no more film, no camera." I thought it sounded like a more complicated explanation than a mugger would sit still for.

"No, no," she said. "In the fantasy he was really nice about it. He was trying to understand me."

We'd both become superstitious as soldiers nearing the end of their tour. Annie's latest blood tests had come back looking suspiciously normal, her antibodies at zero percent. Did lupus go into remission? Was it possible she'd been misdiagnosed? Annie refused to call her doctor. "I don't want to find out I don't have it while we're down here," she reasoned, "because then I will be killed." We got into a debate over what seemed like the legitimate statistical question of whether talking incessantly about our robbery/kidnapping/murder increased or decreased its probability of occurring. Whenever one of us spotted an eyelash on the other's cheek, we'd always dab it off and hold it up on a fingertip to wish on and blow away. Once, after Annie had made her wish, I said, "So at least we're safe for another day."

"Well," she said, "I am."

At a circus party at Mexico City's Planet Hollywood, where showgirls were hitting the dance floor, midgets were shooting pool, and roustabouts were getting into shoving matches, Annie and I got drunk on tequila and confessed our deepest fears to each other, which turned out to be identical: that we would be abducted and Annie raped while I was forced to watch. SEX CRIMES INCREASE had been another recent headline.

"I fear that my failure to act heroically will come between us forever," I said. "You will always blame me and think of me as a coward. It'll destroy our friendship."

"I know!" she cried. "I imagine the same thing, you not being able to do anything, and being ashamed and guilty about it, and *I* feel bad! In the fantasy, as I'm being raped, *I* feel bad for *you*."

"That's nice," I said, made sentimental by tequila. "So, look," I continued, "if you *are* raped while I'm forced to watch, is it going to put a huge damper on our relationship?"

"It'll put a big damper on my *life*."

"Right, right, of course," I said. "Well, mine too. I mean, obviously not as much of one—"

"Unless you're next in line," she said, with a certain gleam in her eye.

I stared at her. "You'd *like* that, *wouldn't* you?" I said. "It—it *titillates* you!"

She cackled delightedly, wriggling and stamping her feet. Annie loved the word *titillate*.

On one of our last nights in Mexico City, Annie had one of her panic attacks about mortality. We'd been watching some science show on TV about the scale of the universe, infinity, and eternity, which always gave her the horrors. Like an idiot, I tried to talk her through it and reason with her, until she pulled the blankets over her head and screamed at me to stop. We turned instead to the more soothing *Anaconda*, which had been on heavy rotation on cable all month. We tried to make things more interesting by placing wagers on the order in which the characters would die. Owen Wilson went first, to no one's surprise; we saw his agonized face bulging in bas-relief from the snake's belly during a swim-by. Annie had the pompous scientist down to die next, but then Jon Voight strangled Owen Wilson's girlfriend with his legs. He tried to kill Jennifer Lopez, too, but was stabbed with a tranquilizer dart by Eric Stoltz, shockingly revived from his wasp-sting-induced coma per Annie's prediction, putting her back in the lead. During a lull in the carnage, Annie asked me: "So, if our trip to Mexico City were a movie, which of us would die, and when?"

"Depends what genre it is," I said. I hoped it would not prove to be a film like *Anaconda*, in which the characters' deaths were a foregone conclusion and the only fun was in seeing who would be next. If it was a *noir*, I knew, I was doomed to die alone, the patsy in this conniving dame's frame-up. "Maybe it's a screwball comedy!" Annie said hopefully. Annie did resemble the quirky, scheming heroines of the '30s more than anyone else I knew. And in a comedy no one would die, except maybe some crotchety aunt who'd leave us millions, and we'd end up bickering happily ever after. At last Jon Voight was swallowed whole, in a POV shot from inside the snake's pulsing gullet.

What's obvious in retrospect, although we would have denied it at the time, is how much fun we were having imagining our own gruesome murders, spooking and riling ourselves up like kids on a sleepover. This is essentially the circus's business: turning all the old primal terrors—being devoured by predators, falling while swinging from one branch to another, being chased by leering men with bottles of seltzer—into little pantomimes of near death and escape to thrill and, yes, titillate us. Professionals literally risk their lives to provide us this sensation. These acts wouldn't be exciting without the real possibility of failure, injury, or death. It's a family-friendly form of human sacrifice: instead of the Hill of the Star or Altar of Forgiveness, the Globe of Death. *Lou must die!*

Of course nobody really wants to see anyone killed at the circus—Jesus, it would traumatize the freaking kids for life—but if you really had *no* interest in seeing anyone hurt, you could always go to a movie or the zoo. What you want is to see someone *nearly* get killed. The circus's real promise, the one it whispers as it tucks you in sick on cotton candy, is: *Not this time.* The tamer sticks his head in the lion's maw and withdraws it, grinning; the acrobats bound unhurt off the net, arms raised in triumph; an old lady lifts a surprisingly taut, supple leg to the barre, defying age, a fantasy of athletic grace. Even Jon Voight's not really dead! Holy shit—the titular snake unexpectedly vomited him back onto the deck of the boat, coated with sputum but alive and gasping for air. It was still anybody's game.

I flew home unkilled from Mexico City with two carry-on items: a black velvet painting of the Devil on the toilet and a single pork rind the size of an open umbrella, both of which Annie had cajoled me into buying. After she'd safely returned to the U.S. she sent me another souvenir: a paper-mache figure she'd made inspired by the *alebrijes* we'd seen in Mexico: a little girl with black-and-white-striped Pippi Longstocking limbs, a polka-dot jumper, curly pink-ribboned pigtails, and a skull for a face. It was not only a Hello-Kitty *memento mori* but a sort of self-portrait.

But in another surprise twist, a *ta-da!* reprieve, the snake spat Annie out again, too. About a month after our trip to Mexico, she was unexpectedly given a clean bill of health. Yeah, that's right, guess what: *no more lupus.* It wasn't in remission; it was just gone. Her doctor shrugged and said that in about 5 percent of cases, the disease "just burns itself out." It's also possible she was misdiagnosed; her odd constellation of symptoms could have been caused by "fifth disease," so called because it's the fifth, and least well known, of the infectious childhood rashes. (Schoolteachers are exposed to a lot of germs.) Annie gets a little touchy when you bring up the lupus scare now, and jealously defends her right to continue fretting about her health. One day, she reminds us, it won't be a false alarm. She didn't return anyone's fifty dollars.

I lost my wedding ring in a pyramid of grapefruit at a grocery store a few months after I flew home—another item on Annie's short list of things for which she will never forgive me. Annie married the juggler, the one she'd run away from to join the circus. They now live in the same cabin where I once photographed her illicitly sitting thumbs-up in vindictive triumph. Not least among his virtues, she explained, was: "He puts up with me." Watching her walk down the aisle to the theme song from *Star Trek: Enterprise*, her ex-fiancé Zach, standing next to me, wept. In an entirely uncharacteristic burst of emotion he admitted, "I always thought I'd end up with Annie." I had never thought any such thing, and yet, looking at the wedding photos, I have to admit I look kind of teary-eyed, too.

Twenty years after the Great Mexico City Circus Train Caper, the Greatest Show on Earth announced that it would be closing after 146 years. Feld Entertainment, which owns the circus, claimed that attendance had dropped after animal rights activists forced them to eliminate elephants from the show. Annie, now a fervid animal rights activist herself, was unmoved: "They were behind the times anyway." It's true the circus was an atavism, a relic of the nineteenth century surviving improbably into the twenty-first, like faith healers still working their tent-revival miracles on satellite. The trapeze and the high wire must seem lame and anachronistic to kids jaded to slow-motion zero-g CGI martial arts. Early movies captured real acts—Douglas Fairbanks scrambling up a drawbridge, the house falling down around Buster, Fred and Ginger doing a once-in-eternity dance in a single take. Most action scenes in American movies are now effectively very expensive cartoons, but the circus was still low-rent and real—muscle and sweat, sawdust and dung, and the chance of blood in the air.

I remember, on my last day in Mexico City, watching the show one last time. When the circus began, they'd bring on everything at once in a motley spangled parade like a Roman triumph, a total sensory onslaught designed to blow the minds of five-year-olds: clowns, acrobats, dancing girls, giant puppets, a whole basketball team on unicycles, camels and zebras, elephants walking single file with tails twined in trunks, the animal tamer in a chariot flanked by tigers. It was the first time I'd given in and watched the circus with uncritical kidlike interest; it gave me chills when the tamer cracked his whip and a team of dappled whites reared up in unison, plumed and rampant. Even the tightrope act seemed more suspenseful than usual. Unlike Annie, I do have a fear of heights, and my stomach clenched with sympathetic terror as I watched the act's climax, a seven-person human pyramid crossing the high wire. I realized I hadn't been breathing only after they'd made it safely to the other side. You could hear the gust of cathartic exhales all around the arena. Then the fanfare and applause. It looked pretty scary there for a while, but see?—everyone's fine. Everybody knows, at least in theory, how to make it to the other side: you just keep placing one foot in front of the other, don't look down, and keep smiling, no matter what. The show, as they say, must go on.

These fantasies of untimely violent death—not just the circus but slasher films, zombie apocalypse, and suicided idols—appeal mostly to children and adolescents. One's own perfectly timely, natural death of unglamorous cancer or unattractive old age is a lot less fun to contemplate. So far, despite our decades of histrionic dread,

Annie and I have both escaped serious illness, injury, or, arguably, any real problems at all. Except, of course, for time. Annie's seriously contemplating cosmetic surgery to address the issue of her incipient "wattle"; I've begun to fear that her vision of my jowls may prove prophetic. Annie's mother died of a stroke a few years ago; mine has Parkinson's. At a little past the actuarial halfway point, we're both starting to suspect that life may not have much left in the way of pleasant surprises in store for us. Annie's lately been having panic attacks, and been prescribed Klonopin, Zoloft, and a beta-blocker, and has started cognitive-behavioral therapy for "death anxiety." The last time we talked she was having trouble swallowing; she was pretty sure it was cancer. *Everybody's got to have something.*

Sometime last winter, in a dark existential hour, I remembered Annie's old emergency antidote to her own late-night dread and decided, *Fine—I'll try it.* The clip that did it for me was the famous last number from *Follow the Fleet*—"Let's Face the Music and Dance." Fred Astaire, busted at the gaming tables on some shipboard casino, deserted by the girls who fawned over him when he was a winner, wanders disconsolately out onto some fantastic gleaming art deco set where he takes out a little silver gun and holds it dramatically to his temple—but then he sees Ginger Rogers, also despondent, slinking out to the rail to throw herself over the side. He stops her and shows her his gun, pantomiming that he was just about to do something foolish himself. She makes a grab for it, but he frowns at her and tosses it over the side. And then he coaxes her to dance. It looks as if he's saving her, but really she's the one who's saved him.

Annie and I still ride the train together. Because of her flying phobia, Annie's racked up so many rail miles on Amtrak that she gets a free sleeper car cross-country once a year and often lets me hop the train with her. We like to take the *Empire Builder* from Seattle to Chicago, hanging out in the observation lounge, watching Glacier National Park and the Great Plains go by with a supply of *New York Times* crosswords and Percocet at hand. What we love most about the train is sort of the same thing we like about painkillers: the cozy in-betweenness of it, being suspended between destinations, temporarily exempt from the relentless press of time. The demographics on a transcontinental train skew so old that, even in our late forties, we get to be the glamorous young couple on board, like newlyweds on honeymoon. Human beings never were more lovely, more perfect in motion.

Kind of Love

Few are lured to the cartooning profession by the promise of its groupie action; it'd be like going into poetry for the money. Most fans of my own strip seemed to be punks or Satanists or bearded conspiracy theorists who brewed their own beer. So when a twenty-four-year-old model contacted me with a friendly, unabashed sexual proposition, it seemed likely to turn out to be either a hoax perpetrated by a basement full of snickering teens or an FBI sting operation based on a spookily astute psych profile. Her online photos made her look like a police sketch of my own anima: a tall, leggy, raucous, loudmouthed girl wearing an eye patch and a pirate hat, hoisting a bottle of whiskey high, her limbs sloppily asplay to expose armpit and pubic hair dyed scarlet. The photos appeared to have been taken at some sort of San Franciscan freak parade; a mock-up of a pirate ship was visible. Other photos showed her nude body painted silver and blue, with vines twining up her torso. In close-ups, you could see a silver spiderweb of fine chains connecting three facial piercings, at nostril, eyebrow, and earlobe.

Her professional name was "Elektra Bold" but her real name, she told me, was Zoey. (Zoey wasn't her real name, either; it was her middle name, which I learned only when I overheard her mother call her Meredith. By then I understood that having penetrated only one name out from her real one was an impressive index of intimacy.) She described herself as a performance artist, fetish model, and "pleasure activist." She had grown up in Baltimore, where my cartoon ran in the local alternative weekly, which she said had helped her get through her depressed adolescence—clinically depressed, as in institutionalization and ECT. She told me a whole long story about her friend Ray and her deciding, during a drunken blizzard in Baltimore, to phone me up and offer to buy me a beer and give me a blow job, respectively. The plan had guttered away with the hangover thaw, and she lived on the West Coast now, but she was writing to tell me she'd be back in Baltimore for a week at Christmas and that her part of the offer, at least, was still valid.

I was much younger then (we met through a now-extinct social network) and my inner fourteen-year-old, still incredulous that girls would consent to get into bed with him at all, was very much alive and exerting considerable influence. Most of my serious girlfriends to date had been what Zoey would call my "type A": smart, pretty, sane, moral girls with glasses who tended to work for nonprofits or write, not bawdy dominatrices. I was tortured by the suspicion that I was missing out on a whole world of evil sexual adventure—threesomes and sex clubs and rampant, unrepentant sluttiness. This out-of-the-ether invitation seemed like my entrée into that world, like a found invitation to an orgy. And after all, this is the whole reason you become an artist in the first place, besides not wanting to get a job: in hopes that it will make girls* want to have sex with you.

"Dude," my friend Harold advised me, after conducting some Internet researches of his own, "I think she might be a whore."

---

* Insert preferred gender/s.

"No, no, no," I said. "She's just one of those free-spirited, West Coast, sex-positive types. I'm pretty sure she's not literally a prostitute."

She was literally a prostitute. Actually, Zoey preferred the term *whore*. She confided this to me a few weeks before we were to meet, with a nervousness that seemed touchingly out of character for her no-prisoners image; she was afraid it might deter me from following through on our date. It did give me pause. I had never patronized a prostitute, less because of any moral qualms than a self-imposed stigma: I didn't want to think of myself as the kind of guy who patronized prostitutes. I also couldn't imagine suspending disbelief enough to convince myself that someone was attracted to me who was being paid to act like it (although I did this easily enough with barmaids, waitresses, baristas, clerks, massage therapists, and psychiatrists). But I wasn't a customer, I reasoned; Zoey really did like me, even if the "me" she liked was as much a professional persona as her own.

The day we met, she came to the door of her mother's house wearing only a towel, still warm and pink from the shower. (Zoey had been running forty minutes late pretty much since birth.) The chains on her face made me a little ill at ease; I couldn't help but imagine someone grabbing them all in a fist and yanking. But the warmth and moisture and steamy, just-out-of-the-shower smell of her when she hugged me hello made her seem very present and fleshly and accessible. Her hair was no longer pirate red but its natural dark brown. She had the thick, dramatic eyebrows of a Russian contessa. I liked that she was as tall as I was. Our talk online had been all wry, knowing innuendo, but now that here we were in real life we were both a little self-conscious about the awkward social situation in which we'd placed ourselves.

I had had several negative experiences with the sexily insane, ranging from stabbing to nonconsensual cohabitation, and so was now guarded in my dealings with them. What made up my mind that Zoey would be safe to get involved with—that, despite her multiple piercings and profligate whiskey swigging and proffering oral sex to strangers on spec, she was not essentially damaged, dangerous, or emotionally disabled—was seeing her with her sister. Her younger sister Bea was a pretty, hippieish high school girl bound for Brown who'd had the same boyfriend throughout high school; the two of them together reminded of me of the split-screen poster for that eighties exploitation movie—"High School Honor Student by Day. Hollywood Hooker by Night." But watching the two sisters dance hand in hand in their living room, laughing at their own silliness and for joy, felt like blundering across something beautiful in the wild—like seeing the courtship flight of hummingbirds, their flickering gemlike bodies rocketing fifty feet into the air and suddenly plummeting.

After Bea and her boyfriend left, Zoey and I were alone in the house. I soon learned that 65 percent of my time with Zoey would be spent waiting for her to get ready—sitting and flipping through a book while she ransacked her suitcase, strewing the room with corsets and boas, strap-ons and camisoles, handcuffs and frilly little underthings. It was less like getting dressed to go out than mounting a production of *Die Walküre*. She chose an ensemble of fence-net stockings, a hat with little cat ears, and an enormous furry purple coat whose name was Violetta* to go to lunch at a pub. Just as I thought we were finally ready to leave, she said coquettishly, "But first, I was thinking we should honor the conditions of our deal."

"Okay, so just tell me," my friend Lauren once asked: "Was the sex with her, like, the best you'd ever had?"

Prurient-minded friends who've plied me for information

* Unknown whether this name was an allusion to the courtesan of *La Traviata*.

about the life of a prostitute are always disappointed by how little I can tell them. It was only in the last year that it even occurred to me to ask Zoey how much she charges. The truth is, I hardly ever asked her about her job, not because it made me jealous or squeamish but for the same reason I hardly ever ask my friend Gabe about his career at NASA, except insofar as it concerns the existence of aliens: talking about work is boring. And however salacious it may seem to civilians, that's what prostitution is: another goddamn job. As in any job, Zoey has good days and crappy ones, clients she looks forward to and some she has to put up with. Although she tries to be careful, she's occasionally found herself in a creepy or dangerous situation. (Driving out the long dirt road to my cabin, she told me: "You realize that if you were a client there is no way in hell I would ever agree to come out here.") She's more conscientious about her sexual health than most amateurs. She's not a runaway or junkie, a sex slave or indentured immigrant; she wasn't abused as a child, doesn't get slapped around by some pimp, and isn't in the business against her will. She went to a posh private school and graduated college. She enjoys her work and considers it a vocation; she describes some of her relationships with clients as truly intimate. Her experience as a prostitute is atypical—it's the equivalent of cultivating craft, small-batch, sustainable marijuana in Telluride as opposed to running dime bags in Baltimore—but Zoey argues that it shouldn't be. Instead of harassing sex workers, she says, governments should be ensuring that more of them are like her: voluntary, safe, and satisfied in their work. Anyway, I'm in no position to disapprove of her profession, even if I were disposed to, since, although I've never been a client, I've certainly been a beneficiary of her skill set.

To keep this essay just barely confined to the realm of literary respectability instead of blooming into unrepentant smut, I'm afraid I'm going to discreetly elide the dirty parts of this story. But because there is simply no understanding certain relationships outside of bed, in respectable daylight, I will say that our week together was not unlike like one of those having-fun-and-getting-to-know-each-other music video montages in a romcom, if they had those sequences in porn films. We parked on a side street in Baltimore with only steamed-up windows for privacy while caterers carried giant bowls of salad right past us. I learned that using Violetta as a blanket was not unlike having a ménage à trois. We practiced very poor road safety. At my isolated cabin I seriously feared that my neighbors, overhearing us, might call the police, mistakenly assuming I was murdering someone.

To answer Lauren's question: it was pretty good. It wasn't that Zoey was privy to any professional sex tricks or ancient tantric secrets so much as her frank, matter-of-fact attitude: *So what do you like to do? Anything you've never tried but always wanted to?* It was a relief to have sex be, for once, unabashedly about the sex itself, instead of feeling like some unspoken promise or a tacit contract with a lot of fine print. Nothing was going to shock or offend her; nothing was weird or taboo. We did some things I had never done before that I'd always wanted to try, which things, it turned out, I liked just as much as I'd suspected I would. (I'm sure my own proclivities seemed boringly ordinary to her; the one time she snuck up behind me and bit me, not lightly, on the ear, I said, "PLEASE DO NOT DO THAT"—and not in the sex voice but in the your-chair-is-on-my-foot voice.) Zoey, who is privy to so many secret predilections, thinks it's a pity that so many people only act out their filthy kinks with professionals or in one-night stands, and are perversely inhibited with the people they love, the same way they'll tell total strangers secrets they hide from their wives.

These are the kinds of intimacies that bond together couples who must seem, to onlookers, inexplicably ill-matched. People seeing Zoey and me together on the street must've assumed either that I'd hired her or that our lives involved a lot of role-play—that the next day, perhaps, she would be dressed in a power suit and I would be wearing a dog collar. For Zoey, every day was like a combination of senior prom and Halloween. I had to get used to being with someone who was a spectacle everywhere we went. It was like being friends with a celebrity, or walking a pet leopard. I once got to watch an entire Sicilian brass band check her out in the frank but courtly Mediterranean manner—each man giving her a leisurely, judicious once-over in turn as we passed, eyebrows raised, lips pursed in appreciation—both more shameless and more civilized than the furtive, sleazy American leer.

My own snobby theory had always been that anyone who needed to go to elaborate lengths to make themselves look interesting must not be. I liked go forth into the world disguised as a grown-up, the better to wrongdo unmolested by the police. But this was of course just as much a costume as Zoey's more theatrical wardrobe; the difference was that whereas my coloration was for camouflage, hers was for display. What I tried to conceal, Zoey advertised. Once when we were drifting in a rowboat in Central Park, Zoey dressed in high Edwardian foppery in honor of Oscar Wilde's birthday, a Conservative Jewish girl of about fourteen called boldly out to her from another boat: "Where are you from?" Zoey answered: "San Francisco," either confirming a lifetime of stereotypes or—who knows?—maybe launching another young soul on the rapids to depravity.

Although all my girlfriends to date had been what Zoey called type A, there was another type I'd always been attracted to, ever since my Byronic crush on tenth-grade poetess Deena Stroehmann, with her feathered bleach-blond hair, suicidal eyeliner, and tight black parachute pants, a type I had never once gotten to go out with: the cool girls, the bad girls, the tough, slutty, rowdy girls, with shocks of fuchsia or cerulean hair, pierced lips and nipples and elaborately tattooed asses; girls who wore ripped-up fishnets with little plaid schoolgirl skirts and silly neon sneakers or combat boots, who had day jobs as barmaids or strippers and sculpted with scrap metal or made guerrilla documentaries, girls who drove muscle cars barefoot while blasting Led Zeppelin. My cartoonish description should make clear how little experience I had actually had with such women. This was the elusive, hitherto hypothetical type B. Now, for the first time, I got to be with one. For me it was a glimpse behind the scenes of something that had always been mysterious, off-limits.

Of course she was a quivering insecure mess inside like everyone else. Her flamboyant coloration was less for sexual display than a kind of protective mimicry—that adaptation whereby a harmless animal imitates a deadly one, pretending to be venomous when all it wants is not to get eaten alive. We both presented deceptively fierce fronts to the world, behind which we were mushily vulnerable. Readers who knew me only through my cartoons expected someone unshaven, apoplectic, and semicoherent with drink; Zoey, a performer, understood that what she "knew" of me was a persona, and enjoyed getting backstage to meet the actual me. And although I was grateful for the entrée that my cartoon alter ego had granted me into her favors, I found I liked the sensation of getting to be known. Lingerie (or leather, or latex) may be more enticing than nudity, but the thrill is still in finding out what's underneath.

I enjoyed camping it up around her in the role of Privileged Straight White Male, or Cynical East Coaster. Zoey and her friends' conversation sounded to me like a pidgin of Queer Theory academese and New Age horseshit: I'd squinch up my face in distaste when she said things like *heteronormative* and *exoticization*, the linguistic equivalent of '70s architecture. Like a lot of West Coasters, she was loath to own up to any unattractive emotions, and would say that someone was "teaching her compassion" rather than that he was "an asshole." It was fun getting to play the straight man, the normal one, since I had so few friends around whom I could plausibly assume this role.

Annoyingly, she never let me get away with it. With the acuity of a con artist spotting a colleague, she quickly sized me up as one of her own kind. She called me a "stealth weirdo." An understanding grew between us that, despite our superficially polar looks, we were essentially the same underneath: self-doubting artists, depressive fuckups, deviants, and freaks. She really was a performance artist—it was not, in her case, a euphemism for *pole dancer*—a sexual provocatrix in the tradition of Annie Sprinkle, letting strangers look at her cervix through a speculum or attempting to get impregnated onstage. We both suffered from bouts of abysmal self-doubt, and each sometimes lay awake at night wondering *Oh, what is to become of me?* Once when I was trying to talk to her in an earnest, concerned-friend way about the relatively short span of a prostitute's earning years, she said, "Thank you for your financial counsel, Mr. Twenty-Dollars-a-Week." I hung my head in shame. When she'd tell me about her byzantine, impossible-to-follow relationship troubles—typically not just love triangles but love rhombi, dodecahedra, or hypercubes—I'd ask her, "So, how's that whole polyamory thing going?" She'd counter: "How's monogamy working out for you?" And we would both hang our heads in shame.

These were just the kinds of differences it's fun to play up between friends, like one of you arbitrarily taking the role of the one who says *I don't know, maybe we shouldn't* and the other the one who says *Aw, c'monnn—what's gonna happen?* That I write and Zoey has sex for a living seems incidental; what's essential is that we're both passionate devotees of our respective vocations. When I was thirteen I wrote up an outline of my future life in which I would be a writer living in a circular house in Montana with a puma whose name would be Ralph; at the same age Zoey drew a picture of the brothel she and her friends would run, called Chez Cécile, all of them lounging invitingly about in negligees.

It was obvious, even to recidivist disaster-seekers like ourselves, that Zoey and I would've self-destructed as a couple almost instantaneously, so we both held back a certain emergency reserve of affection in the interest of self-preservation. I'd hoped that all the obvious obstacles to a "real" relationship with Zoey, among which the fact that she was a prostitute was not even #1, might safeguard me against getting too erotically addicted—or, worse, romantically attached—and spare me the usual NASCAR-like emotional crash.

It mostly worked. There were a couple of uncomfortable moments in just the one week we spent together. She made out with another girl in front of me, a sight that allegedly inflames most hetero dudes to hooting frenzies of lust but mostly made me feel like I ought to excuse myself. She made the mistake of introducing me to one of her other lovers, a person named Pale Eddie. I was not pleased to meet him. I stopped by her house to return a purse she'd left in my car and got to find her in bed with someone else. All these glancing hurts acted as mild, inoculatory doses of jealousy that protected me against what would've been a more virulent case later on. The most jealousy I ever felt over Zoey was when I learned she was seeing another cartoonist—my one meager claim to uniqueness negated. I didn't want to be part of anyone's harem, just another sensual treat to be sampled. "I know," Zoey said when I tried to explain all this for the zillionth time. "You are a special special snowflake."

There was a moment that week when I found myself standing at an I-95 Park & Ride at dusk, waiting to meet a stranger who would sell me some special thermal blankets for Zoey's snakes (she had three, named after the Gorgons) to wear during their cross-country flight to San Francisco. Harold told me over the phone: "Dude, your life has officially become strange."

At the end of our week together, Zoey sat on the edge of her bed and made a touchingly shy speech: "I know I've only known you a week," she said, "and I know we don't really know each other, and I don't want this to sound crazy or anything, but . . . I just want you to know that I've really enjoyed spending this week with you and getting to know you and—whatever it means—I . . . kind of . . . love you."

"I know you do, Zoey," I said. "I kind of love you, too."

Maybe this sounds naïve, as if we were confusing an erotic daze with something more real. Sex is supposedly superficial, merely physical—as though love weren't physical, too, a neural squall of endorphins and hormones. And yet I've noticed that most people can only sleep together casually for so long before they have to admit either that they don't really like each other and have to stop, or else that they really do, and it isn't casual anymore. A woman once told me she loved me on our second date, which made me reflexively wary: she seemed overinvested way too soon. It was years too late before I realized that I'd loved her, too. Who's to say that sex is not as legitimate a way into intimacy as having dinner and drinks and talking about your pets and siblings and favorite films—that it isn't, also, a kind of love? (The King James Bible famously translates the Hebrew word ידע, "to know," to refer to sex.) People who disapprove of prostitution call it "selling your body," but what Zoey was selling was really only a token compared to what she threw in for free. Sex was just the occasion for the real transaction, the way a bar ostensibly sells alcohol but really affords a forum for companionship, conversation, flirting, laughter, and the chance of meeting someone new.

In the *Epic of Gilgamesh*, the king Gilgamesh dispatches Shamhat, a temple prostitute of the goddess Ishtar, to seduce a rampaging "wild man," Enkidu. (Ishtar was the Akkadian name for the planet Venus, which the Greeks and Romans later named after their own sex goddess.) Enkidu, whose epithet is not honorary, fucks her for seven days straight without losing his erection. This has somewhat the same effect on Enkidu that eating the forbidden fruit does on Adam: his old animal pals suddenly get leery of him; he puts on clothes and moves to the big city. He is exiled from the natural world. Except that Gilgamesh was written a thousand years before Genesis, in a religious tradition that didn't pit sex and the sacred against each other, so this isn't some cosmic transgression that fucks over men, women, and snakes forever after. The prostitute awakens Enkidu to his humanity: he learns to understand language, and discovers friendship. She civilizes him.

My seven days with Zoey wrought some similar transformation on me, although I am no Enkidu, and my problem was perhaps that I'd gotten a little *too* civilized, too repressed and polite. Zoey helped undomesticate me. Our whirlwind pornographic romance precipitated a phase in my own life of sexual adventure: the women I would meet in my thirties—installation artists, strippers, and insane German neuroscientists, women with names like Onyx and Fancy and Lady Tenebrae—tended to be less inhibited, more matter-of-fact about letting me know what they wanted. As was I. The archetype of the Sacred Prostitute, in Jungian psychology, still represents the reunion of sex and spirit. Zoey claims this is her true vocation: to help people out of their everyday disguises and let them act, if only for an hour or two, like themselves.

Some men like to argue that hiring a call girl is no different from any other relationship, just more up-front and explicit; they're all essentially transactions, they say. This is the rationale of people who can't imagine any motives other than need, like Objectivists arguing that self-interest is the basis of all morality because they are themselves incapable of any drives beyond the reptilian. Prostitution is not the same thing as a romantic relationship, but maybe, if elevated to an art—a vocation—it can be something more like therapy, a safely bounded surrogate or rehearsal for the real thing. Remembering Zoey's lament that a lot of her clients express sides of themselves that they hide from their wives, I can't help but wish everyone could behave a little more whorishly, shamelessly using each other and letting themselves be used, with love.

Zoey still jealously guards her status as my #1 groupie emeritus; she calls me her "grouper," which I've given up protesting is a large, morose-looking fish. In what she called her Jesus year, thirty-three, she gave up waiting for circumstances to align themselves and went to a sperm bank. She now lives in Berlin with her daughter and, yes, she's still in the same line of work; she occasionally turns up online bound in extremely complicated knots or gets jetted to Switzerland to breastfeed some diapered billionaire. She sometimes frets and second-guesses her career, but then again so do I, and for much the same reasons: it doesn't pay much, there are no benefits, and it often feels like an unrewarding slog. Whenever we talk we get right to the big three a.m. fears: our frustrations as artists, our relationship troubles, our regrets about every life choice we've ever made—*Oh, what is to become of us?* We still tell each other "I love you," and whatever it means, we mean it. The last time I saw her, she came up to my cabin and we sat on my couch watching old episodes of *Dark Shadows*, ate a whole box of fancy chocolates, and painted each other's toenails with shoplifted polish. (Zoey favors brands with names like Pretty Poison and Daddy's Girl.) That polish turned out to be surprisingly durable; I walked the streets of New York for the rest of the winter with my toenails an iridescent peacock blue, their gaudy splendor hidden from view beneath the dull black cover of my wingtips.

Oof

I recently received an email that was about me, but wasn't *for* me; I'd been cc'd by accident. This is one of the hazards of email, reason 697 why the Internet is Bad—the apocalyptic consequence of hitting REPLY ALL instead of REPLY.

I had rented a herd of goats for reasons that aren't relevant here, and had sent out a mass email with attached photographs of my goats to illustrate that (a) I had goats and (b) having goats was good. There turns out to be something primally satisfying about possessing livestock: a man wants to boast of his herd. Most respondents expressed appropriate admiration and envy of my goats, but the email in question, from my agent, was intended as a forward to some of her coworkers, sighing over the frivolous expenditures on which I was frittering away my advance. The word *Oof* was used.

I've often thought that the single most devastating cyberattack a diabolical anarchic mind could devise would not be on the government, the military, or the financial sector, but simply to simultaneously make every email and text ever sent universally public. It would be like suddenly subtracting the strong nuclear force from the universe: the fabric of society would instantly disintegrate, every marriage, friendship, and business partnership dissolved. Civilization, held together by a fragile web of tactful phrasing, polite omissions, and benign lies, would self-destruct in a universal holocaust of bitter recriminations and weeping, breakups and fistfights, divorces, bankruptcies, scandals and resignations, blood feuds and litigation, wholesale slaughter in the streets, and lingering ill will.

This particular email was, in itself, no big deal. Tone is notoriously easy to misinterpret online, and you could've read my friend's message as affectionate headshaking rather than a contemptuous eye roll. It's frankly hard to parse the word *oof.* And to be fair, I *am* terrible with money, unable to distinguish between any amounts other than $∞.00 and $0.00: I always seem to have the former until suddenly and without warning it turns into the latter. But I like to think of this as an endearing foible, or at least no one else's business, rather than imagine that it might be annoying—or, worse, boring—for my friends to have to listen to me bitch about the moribund state of the publishing industry and the digitization of literature while also watching me blow my advance on linen suits and livestock.

What was surprisingly wounding wasn't that the email was insulting but simply that it was unsympathetic. Hearing other people's uncensored opinions of you is an unpleasant reminder that you're just another person in the world and everyone else does not always view you in the forgiving light that you hope they will—making allowances, assuming good intentions, always on your side. There's something existentially scary about finding out how little room you occupy, and how little allegiance you command, in other people's hearts.

This experience is not a novelty of the Information Age; it's always been available to us through the analog technology of eavesdropping. Those moments when you overhear others describing you without censoring themselves for your benefit are like catching a glimpse of yourself in a mirror without having first combed your hair and correctly arranged your face, or seeing a candid photo of yourself online, not smiling or posing but just looking the way you apparently always do, oblivious and mush-faced with your mouth open. I've written essays about friends that I felt were generous and empathetic but that they experienced as devastating. I've also been written *about*, in ways I had no factual quarrel with but that nonetheless made me wince to read. It is simply not pleasant to be objectively observed. It's proof that you are visible, that you are *seen*, in all your naked silliness and stupidity.

Needless to say, this makes us embarrassed and angry and damn the people who've thus betrayed us as vicious two-faced hypocrites. Which in fact everyone is. Gossiping and making fun of each other are among the most ancient and enjoyable of human amusements. And we should really know better than to confuse this with true cruelty. Of course we make fun of the people we love: they are ridiculous. Anyone worth knowing is inevitably also going to be complicated, difficult, and exasperating—making the same obvious mistakes over and over, squandering their money, dating imbeciles, endlessly relapsing into dumb addictions and self-defeating habits, blind to their own hilarious flaws and blatant contradictions and fiercely devoted to whatever keeps them miserable. (And those people about whom there is nothing ridiculous are the most ridiculous of all.) It is necessary to make fun of them in order to take them as seriously as we do. Just as teasing someone to his face is a way of letting him know that you know him better than he thinks, that you've got his number, making fun of him behind his back is a way of bonding with your mutual friends, reassuring each other that you both know and love and are driven crazy by this same person.

Although sometimes—let's admit it—we're just being mean. A friend of mine described the time in high school when someone walked up behind her while she was saying something clever at that person's expense as the worst feeling she had ever had. And not just because of the hurt she'd inflicted, but because of what it forced her to see about herself: that she made fun of people all the time—people who didn't deserve it, who were beneath her in the social hierarchy—just to make herself seem funny or cool or to ingratiate herself with other girls.

A friend once shared with me one of the aphorisms of twelve-step recovery programs: "What other people think of you is none of your business." Like a lot of wisdom, this at first sounds suspiciously like nonsense: obviously what other people think of you is your business; it's your main job in life to try to micromanage everyone's perceptions of you and do tireless PR and spin control for yourself. Every woman who ever went out with you must pine for you. The ones who rejected you must regret it. You must be loved, respected—above all, taken seriously! Those who mocked you will *rue the day*!

The problem is that this is insane—the psychology of dictators who regard all dissent as treason, and periodically order purges to ensure total, unquestioning loyalty. Eventually a mob is going to topple your statues. The operative fallacy here is that unconditional love means not seeing anything negative about someone, whereas it really means pretty much the opposite. (In the story "Rebecca," about a woman with green skin, Donald Barthelme writes: "Do I want to be loved *in spite of*? Do you? Does anyone? But aren't we all, to some degree?") We don't give other people credit for the same interior complexity we take for granted in ourselves—the same capacity for holding contradictory feelings in balance, for complexly alloyed affections, for bottomless generosity of heart and petty malice. We can't believe that anyone could be unkind to us and still be genuinely fond of us, although we do it all the time.

I finally had a talk with my agent about the Oof faux pas, in which, as so rarely happens, we actually got down to the real tension underlying our tiff. As usual, it had less to do with me than I'd imagined. It is, after all, my agent's job to make money for me, but because I am as oblivious and self-absorbed as most people, the possibility that she might've interpreted my recreational complaining as a reproach had never occurred to me. That accidental glimpse of unguarded feeling had clarified and deepened our friendship. In the end, all parties apologized, reiterated their mutual affection and respect, and formally acknowledged the environmental and economic benefits of goats over mowing. It may be that it's less exchanged favors or compliments than hurt feelings and fights that turns us into intimates. Months later I sent her a photo of myself at the Museum of Modern Art, glowering next to Ed Ruscha's painting of the word OOF.

A friend of mine once had a dream about a strange and terrible device: a staircase you could descend deep underground, in which you heard recordings of all the things anyone had ever said about you, both good and bad. The catch was, you had to pass through all the worst things people had said first before you could get to the best things said about you, at the very bottom. This wasn't even my dream, and my friend told me about it over a quarter century ago, but I've never forgotten it. There is no way I would make it more than two and a half steps down such a staircase, but the dream-metaphor is clear enough: if you want to enjoy the rewards of being loved, you also have to submit to the mortifying ordeal of being known.

Our War on Terror

Political movements, protests and revolutions have always attracted romantics. Lauren and I were both cartoonists, who, as a genus, fail to abandon their childish enthusiasms and are undaunted by an endeavor's self-evident futility. We met at a comic-book signing, events that tend to be all lull. At one of the slower moments, Lauren, who was one of the featured artists, gave me a sly sizing-up look from behind her table, over where I was slouched on the floor with my back against the wall. "So, Tim," she asked: "what's your deal?"

We were each a little exotic to the other: she was a cool, grungy riot grrl from the Pacific Northwest, and, she told me later, she saw me as one of those moneyed, well-mannered East Coast prep-school boys she'd read about growing up, boys who were sensitive and read books—"not like the horrible boys of real life." In her first letter to me she wrote: "I knew right away that I wanted to be your friend."

Back then, circa 1998, if you saw a minicomic or zine you admired, you'd write the artist a letter, and a week or so later maybe they'd write back. It was like radioing messages back and forth between star systems. Lauren's and my correspondence was intimate right away, by which I mean not erotic or flirty but frank and confiding, dispensing with the bullshit and getting right down to matters of art, life, and the Big Questions. Like me, Lauren had committed herself to the impoverished and marginal life of an artist, and we commiserated over the Herculean feat of sitting down and beginning something, the need to practice a slogging routine while waiting for inspiration, and the shame, and illicit pleasures, of procrastination. She wrote about ambivalence: ambivalence about quitting her day job to draw comics full-time, about the worthwhile struggle of monogamy and marriage, about whether or not to have children ("Fuck motherhood!" she wrote in a passing moment of resolve). Our letters were stuffed with gifts: our smartest thoughts, unworthiest emotions, incidents and details curated to amuse. Whenever we met at conventions or expos we'd boringly hog each other's company, ignoring roomfuls of colleagues to yak all night.

Lauren and her husband, Lars, and I all moved to New York City in the winter of 2000, where we got to be friends off paper, out in real life. Lauren and I went on long walks, hung out in each other's apartments, went to art films and galleries and museums together, had greasy diner lunches and afternoon tea, big Szechuan dinners and countless beers. It was at an exhibit called *Surrealism: Desire Unbound* at the Metropolitan Museum of Art, where Lauren mocked Dalí's lobsterphone and we laughed at all the photos of bourgeois middle-aged artists in three-piece suits picnicking with naked ladies—the placards repeatedly described the Surrealists as "whisking away" young models to be their "muses"—that it occurred to me, with something like alarm, that there was no one in the world I would rather be there with than Lauren. Afterward we sat out on a steep, grassy slope behind the Met and talked about Edward Albee's *The Goat, or Who Is Sylvia?*, a tragic farce about a man in love with an unlikely object, and about my transgender friend Jenny, who'd had to explain something that seemed just as absurd and indefensible to her own family—about passionate, irrational, ruinous love, something we'd both experienced first-hand. I'd dressed up in slacks and a shirt and silk tie that day, because it was Laundry Day, and I had nothing worse to wear. When I'd met Lauren on the steps of the Met, she exclaimed, "You look gorgeous!" No one had ever called me *gorgeous* before.

After my first winter in New York, I accidentally called my girlfriend, whose name was not Lauren, "Lauren." She asked me directly whether I was in love with Lauren, and I assured her that of course I wasn't—we were just friends. It was a meaningless slip of the tongue, a little neural misfire. I, at least, believed me. Once, when Lauren and Lars and I were in a bodega, she called him by my name and got all flustered. Lars said to me, "I'm just not even going to think about what that means." The names of the people we love all seem to be stored in the same compartment of the brain, kept separate from more ordinary words but easily jumbled among one another, as if they're all just different words for the same thing. I've read that endearments, along with song lyrics and curses, can withstand even the ablation of aphasia, like a handful of jewels left intact in a safe after the building around them has been demolished.

It'd be easy to misremember that year as a last idyll before it all slid over the brink, like the summer of 1914. But in truth the nineties were a sordid and trivial decade in which our gravest national crisis was an act of unconstitutional fellatio. It's little remembered now that one of the main issues in the 2000 election, on the eve of a barbarian attack on the capital, was prescription drug benefits. By that late, dynastic stage of empire, the hereditary candidates—one a president's son, the other a senator's—seemed almost interchangeable. So we were torpid and slow to react when the Republicans, in a historic display of poor sportsmanship, declined to accept the results of the election and just stole it, clumsy and unembarrassed as a junkie holding a gun to your girlfriend's head.

The morning of the inauguration I realized I couldn't stand

not to register my impotent protest and took a train from New York to D.C. to go stand in the freezing rain and jeer. News stories the next day catalogued some of the items thrown at the presidential motorcade: an egg, a tennis ball, some ice, an orange peel. I had always resisted drawing overtly topical cartoons, but the week of the inauguration I ran one titled "*What If* . . . Some IDIOT Became the President???" My friend Felix was cast as unlikely commander in chief, his desk littered with bongs and comic books, as an aide burst into the Oval Office crying, "Mr. President the *Russians* are at it again!" Felix, eyes dilated and glassy, clutches his head in his hands as if to keep it from imploding and says, "SWEET weeping Jesus what do we do." I drew this cartoon in January of 2001, eight months before the scene depicted would come to pass.

I experienced the event now known only by its numeric date, as if too terrible to be named, in the same way most of my compatriots did—on television—and reacted the same way so many of them did—by going temporarily insane. A hundred miles from the city, in my isolated cabin, I wanted to see those responsible nuked, their shithole paradise turned into a vast flat rink of Trinitite that would glow faintly at night for the next thirty thousand years to remind the world that the Americans were not to be fucked with. I later noticed that most of the people who went conspicuously berserk with gung-ho bloodlust had experienced the attacks as a TV event, fiery Act I of a formulaic Hollywood blockbuster whose climax had to be the inevitable Act III: Spectacular Payback.

It wasn't until I went to New York a few days later that I realized how misplaced, how grotesquely inappropriate a response this was, like showing up drunk and picking fights at a funeral. Riding the escalator up out of Penn Station, having seen the newly mutilated skyline for the first time, that vast absence ghastly as an amputation, I tried to arrange my expression into a New York face, blank and unapproachable, and failed so completely that a girl on the escalator next to me started crying and embraced me. In the streets, the faces of New Yorkers were heartbreakingly unguarded, like mollusks with their shells torn off, gelid and flinching at the unfamiliar air.

Late that night, draped over chairs in her living room in Brooklyn drinking tumblers of Irish whiskey, Lauren and I sat up long after Lars had gone to bed, talking. She told me her mother, back in Seattle, had cried over the phone that week. "That's what the terrorists accomplished," she said. "I mean, besides the actual deaths, and the grief—that's the worst thing they did: they made everyone in the world feel like shit." Her reaction was so innocent that it shamed me back to sanity. My contempt for the bellicose hysteria of my fellow Americans would always be the more unforgiving because I'd briefly felt it myself, the way we bitterly renounce infatuations or faiths we've outgrown.

Our conversation that night had the raw, punchy honesty of talk at last call, or a wake. Outside her window, across the river, the island of Manhattan was still a crime scene south of Fourteenth Street. TV vans were jammed up and down Eleventh Avenue, their antennae craning like rubberneckers at a car wreck. Downtown, near the relief tents, piles of exhausted firefighters were sacked out on the sidewalks like litters of kittens. The only planes in American airspace that night were military jets. Somewhere out in the darkened continent, our callow new president was in hiding. War was in the air. We didn't know exactly who the war would be with yet, but we knew that soon, sometime in the next few months, thousands of people somewhere in the world were going to die. You could feel History all around you, not an abstraction but alive and dangerous, like an epidemic.

Lauren talked about Pearl Harbor that night, how we look back on it now as the first chapter of a story so familiar it seems a foregone conclusion: *A day that will live in infamy*, the assembly lines retooling from Fords to Superfortresses, D-day and Hiroshima, the sailor kissing the girl in Times Square. But this narrative is only inevitable in retrospect; back then, no one knew how history was going to turn out. There were plenty of isolationists and pacifists in this country before December seventh, and there were still some afterward; they've just been airbrushed out of the textbooks. People then were exactly as frightened and clueless as we were now, unable to see even an instant in front of them, taking uncertain stands for whatever seemed right at the time.

As usual, the people who stepped confidently forward with answers in the crisis were either idiots or villains—*the best lack all conviction, while the worst* you know the rest. Earlier that afternoon I'd eaten lunch at a Polish diner where I saw some politician or think-tank wonk on TV explaining that the terrorists had attacked us because "they hate our freedom." It sounded uncannily like a line from the '70s *Battlestar Galactica* series describing the evil alien Cylons. *Jesus, I thought—is* this *what it's going to be like?* It seemed as if, sometime in that gluttonous, concupiscent Clintonian interlude between the Cold War and this new one, the body politic had gotten so flaccid and atrophied that we could only understand anything in cartoonishly stupid terms.

I had, of course, seen nothing yet.

When any nation-state decides to attack another, the sequence of events is as predictable as the etiology of a disease. Thucydides, writing twenty-four centuries ago, dryly catalogues how the meanings of words are perverted so that recklessness becomes courage, prudence cowardice, and moderation unmanly. In the years of the War on Terror we all learned Orwellian new locutions like *extraordinary rendition* (kidnapping), *enhanced interrogation techniques* (torture), and *misled* (the lie that we weren't being lied to). The government branded the unconnected countries they'd targeted "the Axis of Evil," a comic-book locution like the Legion of Doom. The word *freedom* became so soiled by abuse it could never be spoken by anyone without ignoble motive again.

Hermann Goering, in captivity, was wearily candid about how you get ordinary shlubs to go to war: just tell them your intended target is planning to attack you, and denounce the pacifists as unpatriotic. When administration officials invoked spy-movie scenarios of "a ticking time bomb in Times Square" or a mushroom cloud over Manhattan, the Gulf of Tonkin might as well have been Jenkins' Ear or Helen of Troy for all the American people seemed to know. The intelligentsia, inasmuch as there was such a thing in the twenty-first-century United States, were condemned as effete, craven elitists—"the blame-America-first crowd" or "Bush-haters." Solemn columnists came out of the closet as apologists for torture, a position that would have sounded, only a year or two earlier, like being pro-rape. No one on TV or in print seemed willing to risk saying anything sane or true for fear of being called traitors, cowards, or faggots. One administration insider, deranged by hubris, declared the concept of "reality" naïve and obsolete. The dissonance between official reality and your own fugitive perceptions was so complete that it was easy to feel as if it was you, not the rest of the country, who had gone insane. It all felt less like the usual glum defeat of having the other party in power than some unprecedented historical aberration, a brutal discontinuity with the America we had grown up in. "I almost can't bear to think of it," Lauren wrote me, "that America is being led into the first truly preemptive war in its history by an unelected leader."

It was, at least, great material. Along with military contractors and the petrochemical industry, satirists were among the few beneficiaries of what the administration was calling "the War on Terror." After 9/11 I felt morally conscripted into becoming a political cartoonist; it felt unconscionable to draw cartoons about anything else, given even the marginal public forum of an alternative weekly newspaper. Being a cartoonist during the Bush administration was like being a landscape painter at Krakatoa: each day brought some new affront to common sense or human decency as comedic fodder; the people in power were a rogues' gallery of grotesques out of *Dick Tracy*. The most incredible character of them all was the president himself, feckless and entitled as any child-king, a swaggering malaprop with a fondness for military costume. It was commonly assumed he was a figurehead controlled by his vice president, one of his dad's old cronies, who looked like a caricature of a corrupt industrialist by George Grosz—a bald, snarling oil baron with a mechanical heart.

I still remember the first news story that cheered us up after 9/11: a funeral director in the Atlanta area had literally let his work pile up, secretly stacking dozens of bodies in the woods out behind his funeral home. Lauren and I, both chronic procrastinators, liked to think of this as a simple Failure to Deal on a horrific scale. We imagined him telling himself that this outdoor-storage thing was just a stopgap measure, strictly temporary, waking up every morning and groaning *Ugh, I* really *gotta get on top of this situation*—first thing *Monday, I* swear *to* God. In those days, this is what constituted comic relief.

In early 2002, as the Bush administration was cramming a suspiciously well-prepared three-hundred-page package of legislation through Congress under the dystopian name of "the Patriot Act," Lauren and I organized a "statement of conscience" to be placed in the *Comics Journal*, then the definitive publication of comics news and criticism. It was modeled on a famous diptych of ads that had run on facing pages of *Galaxy Science Fiction* magazine in 1968, in which the science-fiction authors of the era had declared themselves in opposition to or support of the Vietnam War.* Ours was a three-line statement of opposition to the Patriot Act and the

* Interestingly, all of my favorite sf authors were on the con side. Maybe, as with Lauren and the War on Terror, what we believe is inextricable from what we love.

imminent invasion of Iraq that concluded: "If comics have taught us anything, it's that superpowers should be used only for good." Beneath it ran five columns of names, like a splash page of the assembled Justice League.

Placing an ad in a magazine is not self-immolation or a hunger strike, but opening yourself up to public invective and ridicule is nonetheless a bonding experience. Lauren and I had long ago made a pact never again to read any comments on the *Comics Journal*'s message board, the electronic bathroom wall of the comics community, but reactions to our ad inevitably seeped around our firewall. Responses were not unpredictable: the administration's talking points and propaganda slogans were repeated verbatim; certain historical analogies too obvious to mention were invoked; phrases like *real men* and *balls* recurred with unselfconscious frequency. I retain a vivid mental image, evoked by one commenter, of Lauren and myself bending over in submission to receive Iraqi fighter jets up our liberal peacenik asses.

One of the frustrations of being attacked by a decentralized terrorist network is that it isn't immediately clear whom to bomb, which may be one reason Americans turned our thwarted rage against each other. It was as if we'd all been waiting for decades for an excuse to hate each other's guts: conservatives let rip their long-stockpiled loathing of us East Coast ivory-tower eggheaded elitists, and we finally got to unveil our contempt for those dumb gullible gung-ho fuckheads back in flyover country. The general sense in New York City, one of the only places in the country that had actually been attacked, was that out in America everyone had gone apeshit. A lot of barroom conversations among my friends in those days ended by abandoning discourse altogether, growling in frustration at the futility of rational argument in the face of moronic power. We said things like "Let's stop talking about it," "I can't even take it," and "Just *fuck* those fucking fuckers." I overheard a woman at a sidewalk café—a respectable-looking taxpayer, with a stroller—wonder aloud, not especially sotto voce, "Why someone doesn't just do a drive-by" on the president of the United States.

In a time of furious absolutes, anyone in the middle gets shouted down and told to shut up. I drew a cartoon of myself standing between the credulous, dewy-eyed hippies of the Left and the militant imbeciles of the Right, sheepishly holding a protest sign with an illegibly long, prolix slogan, full of qualifications and caveats, with addenda and footnotes that had to be appended to the bottom of the sign with tape. While the government was preparing to topple the Taliban, Lauren had said she wasn't sure she could wholeheartedly join a rally for "peace": "What would that even mean?" Embracing uncertainty and ambivalence had always been one of the shared convictions (if you can call ambivalence a conviction) on which our artistic and intellectual camaraderie was predicated. We both understood that you could hardly ever know for sure that you were right, but in the world you had to act as though you did—always preserving, for integrity's sake, an eternal flame of doubt in the back of your mind, never completely dismissing the possibility that you were full of shit. One night before an antiwar rally, painting signs on my apartment floor, we just about wept with laughter thinking up uninspiring slogans like GIVE APPEASEMENT A CHANCE and THEY PROBABLY DON'T HAVE NUCLEAR WEAPONS.

Lauren and I always went to protests together, because neither of us really liked them. People seem to get stupider in geometric proportion to their numbers, and I hate being asked to chant things like *Hey, hey, ho, ho.* And we knew that none of it would make any difference—or so we told ourselves, over and over, as a kind of preventative incantation to spare ourselves any more painful disillusionment than we'd already suffered. But we did it, firstly, because we couldn't bear to do nothing: that whole decade felt like being held down and spit on by playground bullies, and you couldn't just passively lie there—you owed it to yourself to at least thrash around and scream. And we did it for the same reason we'd run that ad: out of a square, old-fashioned notion that dissent is one of the responsibilities of citizens in what was still, ostensibly, a republic. But mostly, I think, we did it out of a conviction that was more artistic than political, one so indefensible you'd have to call it faith: that it matters when the truth is spoken, even if no one listens.

We had self-consciously dowdy code names that we used for communiqués about our antiwar activities: she was Beryl Pankhurst; I was Obadiah Blott. Lauren, who'd studied political activism in college, believed that our cause was best served by dressing as conservatively as possible instead of confirming the usual lefty stereotypes. She'd been cultivating a frumpy-old-lady look ever since her days back in grunge-era Seattle (whenever she walked down St. Marks Place in the East Village, where kids were still dressing up as Mohawked punks circa 1978, she'd secretly think: I'm *punker than* they *are*) and armored herself for street protests in a cardigan, skirt, and granny glasses. And I was happy for any excuse to wear a suit. I even took to wearing an American flag lapel pin in a futile effort to reclaim that symbol from the warmongers who'd appropriated it. Our protest signs were similarly traditionalist—WORLD DOMINATION IS UN-AMERICAN, scolded one of Lauren's slogans; INVASION IS FOR NAZIS AND MARTIANS said mine, illustrated with swastikas and tentacles—appealing to a peaceable prewar America that was as selectively imagined as conservatives' false memory of some bygone God-fearing white man's paradise.

We were not inconspicuous among the lip rings and dreadlocks, fake tribal tattoos and big rasta hairbags of our allies. One pallid, zaftig Wiccan told us in all earnestness that it was "good to see some normals here." We often marched with a casket-sized American flag stretched between us, and one guy sneered, "Why are you carrying *that*?" at us, as if we were displaying the Stars and Bars. I remember a dude standing atop a flatbed truck draped with Palestinian flags, bellowing over a PA system, "WHAT DO WE WANT?"—to which we were to respond, in Nuremberg unison: "PEACE!!!" Al Sharpton* took his turn at the mike at one rally to demand that someone "Free Mumia!"—a cause that had become shorthand, for Lauren and me, for the Left's easily distracted agenda. At one march I had a fit of despairing laughter and had to sit down on a curb after seeing a sloppily Magic Markered sign that urged the world to SMOKE WEED under a scrawled marijuana leaf that looked like a child's hand-outline picture of Turkey Lurkey.

We were not among those who chained themselves to fences or contrived to get dragged into paddy wagons as acts of passive resistance; we were lazy, craven, dilettantish activists. We had a strict no-jail pact. The closest either of us came to getting arrested was when I was briefly detained by the police for sketching the permed and wattled delegates at the Republican National Convention in New York, but the semiotic squid ink of my suit and NIXON button allowed me to slip free. When we saw a tense confrontation developing between protesters and police under the solemn watch of the marmoreal lions on the steps of the Forty-Second Street library, we exchanged a glance and deployed our prearranged fallback plan: time to get dinner. We arranged to divide our activities at the RNC protests so as to focus on each of our respective areas of interest: in the morning we went to a labor protest so that Lauren could ogle machinists, and in the afternoon we attended a "mass panty flash" by an organization called the Axis of Eve so I could ogle guerrilla exhibitionists. During a march on Washington, Lauren, a big Founding Fathers fangirl, insisted we detour to the Treasury Building to see the salaciously tight-panted statue of Alexander Hamilton, whom she had once drawn making out with Thomas Jefferson.

---

* A preacher/media personality who inserted himself into a number of high-profile events and causes.

After the march in Washington had dispersed, we sat trading swigs from a flask of whiskey on a bench in Lafayette Park, across the street from the black iron fence enclosing the White House and a barricade of black-armored cops bristling with guns and truncheons. "I think we can expect to see some major policy changes very shortly," I said. "Oh, yeah," Lauren agreed. "We truly stuck it to the Man today."

Lauren was not only my comrade in arms through those years but my closest artistic confidante. My main contribution to the antiwar effort was drawing political cartoons, perhaps the purest imaginable exercise in futility; the last time a cartoonist had any actual effect on U.S. politics we still had a bearded president. Through long conversations and reading each other's work and the pleasure-center buzz of her admiration and laughter, Lauren both honed and gentled my art. We always called the president "George," with a kind of weary familiarity, the tone you'd use to talk about an exasperating friend or unhousebroken pet. Although in real life I reacted with such instant and visceral loathing to the sound of the president's voice that I would lunge across the room to snap off the radio whenever he spoke, in my cartoons George became a figure of fun—a hapless, unbright little guy who dimly apprehended that he was in way over his head, like a rhesus monkey at the helm of a crashing starship. He unfailingly called his vice president "Mr. Cheney," the way you'd address your parents' friends as a kid. They became a comic duo, like Laurel and Hardy, Mr. Cheney forever growling, "Geoooooorge!" in frustration. As I drew George's face, I could feel my own features twisting and cringing in involuntary sympathy with the fear and eagerness to please I saw there, the deeply hidden insecurity of the bully.

Maybe it was a kind of Stockholm syndrome, this perverse identification with the man who held us all hostage to his churlish whim. I would've quashed it if I could, but Lauren said it was this weird empathy that kept my cartoons from being agitprop, that gave them a depth and humanity that the more one-sided polemicists of the Left lacked. She'd always shared my terrible pity for Richard Nixon, who'd resigned when we were little kids; after I drew a cartoon called "Li'l Nixon," about the ex-President's early years—lying about eating a Fudgsicle, listening at a wall with a drinking glass, in seclusion in his tree house—she wrote me rhapsodically: "I don't want any cartoons but Li'l Nixon."

I saw her as someone very much like myself, but just a little saner, kinder, wiser. Our minds were the same size, with roughly the same ratios of ambivalence to conviction, cynicism to sentiment. But Lauren seemed capable of moral outrage without rancor, a disappointment in her fellow Americans that didn't descend to contempt. She was as angry as I was, but for better reasons: when the first ugly photos came out of Abu Ghraib prison—U.S. soldiers grinning and giving the thumbs-ups over piles of naked prisoners on leashes—Lauren wept at the thought of all the men and women in uniform who'd ever tried to behave honorably and were now disgraced by association. "We don't get to be the good guys anymore," she said, with irony, rue, and sadness. When the war turned into the quagmire the Bush administration had assured us it wouldn't, Lauren simply mourned the pointless loss of life, while I was secretly relieved that they hadn't been able to repeal the law of cause and effect as easily as the Bill of Rights. It always made me feel better to be around her—*better* in the sense of calmer and more clearheaded, but also like a more decent human being.

There was a thing she would do on our long walks on the sidewalks of Brooklyn or the beach at my cabin: she'd be trying to articulate some complex or knotty thought and suddenly stop, refusing to take another step until she'd worked it out into words. Sometimes I'd casually try to resume our forward progress, but she wouldn't budge until she'd finished what she had to say. I never knew whether she was thinking so hard that her brain could no longer run both operations at once, or if she was doing it for rhetorical emphasis, the perambulatory equivalent of smacking the podium. It reminded me of the way she had in conversation of fixing me with a fishy look to call me on some glib bullshit. She told me once that she worried that my caricatures of our fellow Americans in the red states—what I called "the Shithead Vote," those fat-assed, mustachioed suburban dads with wraparound shades and NASCAR caps, dingbats in belted pantsuits and lacquered bouffants—were too broad and cruel, that I just wasn't being fair. She objected to my cartoon contrasting "the Ladies of the Left" (modeled on the lissome agents of the Axis of Eve) with "the Ladies of the Right" (haggish pro-lifers with dismembered-fetus photos), arguing that I was equating virtue with beauty.

The first time I ever drew Lauren in a cartoon, we had to sit down over beers and have a little talk. Lauren admitted that she had not been initially thrilled to see herself looking, in my depiction, "like a batty old lady." But, she admitted, there was a certain batty-old-ladyish side to her personality, and, as a cartoonist herself, she could understand that I must have observed her carefully, and with great affection, to have captured that aspect of her. She'd often teased me for having such an obvious "type," to which, she had noted, she did not conform. "You like them *wil*-lowy," she'd croon, "with looonnng *tresses*." Lauren herself had chin-length brown hair, and had once told me she'd always thought of herself as "short and stumpy" compared to her pretty, popular older sister.

I did not even make eye contact during this talk, and I'm sure she took my silence as acquiescence. The only thing I could think of to say in response was something I could not say: that her face was my favorite sight on earth. That my heart lit up like the tree at Rockefeller Center every time she walked into a diner or bar to meet me, every time I heard her answer the phone "Tiiim!" with such audible pleasure. That I adored the broad curve of her lip, her pigtails, her knit cap, her leopard coat, the pale blue of her eyes. That I cherished the sly sidewise look she'd give me to let me know when I was full of shit; the way her lower lip pulled to the left when she felt conflicted or guilty; the glances she'd give me across the room at parties, both of us complicit in the knowledge that we'd rather be talking to each other. That sometimes I'd close my eyes and breathe in the air she'd walked through. One rainy afternoon, when I was helping her with some scanning and Photoshop during a deadline crunch, she got up to fetch us some lunch and paused behind me for a moment to rub my left shoulder blade. I felt her handprint there for years.

It was true that I'd at first assumed I was safe from the usual disastrous romantic complications with Lauren, not only because she was married but because she wasn't my type. But those very limits were what allowed love to sneak up on me incognito until it was too late. My useless love for her persisted throughout flings and affairs with other women, some of them deliriously distracting. At times, between my secret love for Lauren and my sex life with someone else, I had what amounted to one whole relationship. The night Lauren and I laughed so hard painting protest signs on my floor was only a week or two after I'd consummated my decades-long crush on the willowy, long-tressed Kati Jo. Even as I walked around New York in a state of ecstatic stupefaction over Kati with Ella Fitzgerald on repeat in my heart, some small, obdurate part of me knew that I would still rather talk with Lauren. What Lauren had to say about my romance with Kati Jo was: "I'm not seeing a lot of winning for you here." In her last letter to me, Kati told me that she couldn't be with me because she knew she'd never be the woman I loved most.

I should make clear that this love affair was confined entirely to my own head. How Lauren may have felt about me is not for me to say; it really isn't even any of my business. I was, of course, wild to know. I scrutinized her for clues, parsed our conversations for subtext. We once had a very delicate conversation about what she thought was the fact that I just wasn't attracted to her. She acted matter-of-fact about it: she knew she wasn't my type, and it wasn't an issue anyway, since she was married. She told me that she loved me as a friend and that she was attracted to me, "so you can imagine how I would feel about you if I weren't married." One morning, when we'd slept in the same room before some march on Washington—her in the bed and me on the floor—I woke up early and thought I'd caught her watching me. But she closed her eyes so quickly I could never be quite sure I'd really seen it.

At the time, falling in love with Lauren seemed unrelated to the protests and the war, but in memory they are inextricable. Veterans and journalists have written about the illicit joys of war: its addictive intensity, its exhilaration and beauty, how it calls up what's finest in people as well as what's base, bonding comrades as unbreakably as family. It has some of the same effect, more faintly and distantly, on civilians—and not just on those flabby Rambo fanboys who wear camo pants to infiltrate the aisles of Target or drive Tonka-yellow Humvees on the deadly road to Muvico. Those of us protesting the war were infected with some of that dreadful excitement, too—a sense of urgency and portent, that our actions mattered as if on some moral battlefield. We got to feel like a brave, embattled band taking a stand for what was right, racing against Armageddon. It's exciting to imagine that you're living at some crucial historic turning point instead of just another unexceptional year in the annals of brutality. It was, in a way, fun, just as it must've been for the planners of the war, a bunch of aging draft dodgers playing Napoleon. Lauren and I got to act out our banal domestic drama against the colossal operatic backdrop of the capital of a collapsing empire. It was an antiwartime romance.

I waited for years for my infatuation to blow over, managing it like a chronic illness. But suppression only sustains and intensifies passion instead of letting it peter out into domesticity, the way the narrow glass canyons of Manhattan Venturi the winds to a pitch that rips umbrellas inside out. Kati Jo used to say she wished Lauren and I could just fuck so I'd get it out of my system, but I never wanted anything as feasible as an affair. I never imagined that Lauren might leave her husband, or entertained shameful little daydreams about his death. The only scenario I could plausibly picture that would bring us together was not Lars's death but my own: I would contract some painless terminal illness that would entitle me to ask Lauren to sit at my bedside in my last months and read to me or bring me little sandwiches. I couldn't envision any realistic way of changing this world; what I wanted was to live in a different one. I was never really a reformer, but a utopian.

On the eve of the 2004 election, Lauren cajoled me into going with her to Pennsylvania to volunteer for the Democratic campaign. The candidate, an august stuffed shirt who was husband to a Mozambican ketchup heiress, inspired a kamikaze fervor among liberals that was 100 percent anti-Bush in origin. On our first day in Philadelphia, Lauren and I were dispatched to carry out the critical mission of standing on a median strip, holding signs and leaping up and down in order to exhort passing drivers to honk. We were a little chagrined about leaping being our contribution to the electoral effort, but also had to admit that leaping was kind of fun. Philadelphia was a Democratic stronghold where we were surrounded by young volunteers, all of us giddy with the feeling that this might really be it, the end of the nightmare Bush years, plus everybody was honking! "Are you kidding?" one guy said to us that night when we were knocking on doors to get out the vote. "I'd vote for *Joe Donut* over George Bush." I let down my pessimistic defenses. As the polls closed I dropped Lauren off at 30th Street Station: she'd said she felt she should watch the returns at home, with Lars. I said I understood. We said we'd be thinking of each other.

You already know how this turned out, but bear in mind that we, trapped in the year 2004, did not. That night in Philadelphia a friend of mine and I numbly watched as the networks called state after state for George. When the Democratic candidate conceded, even unflappable ironist Jon Stewart* looked like he might be about to cry. I later heard that the morning after the election some

* Host of a popular satirical news show.

despondent liberal had gone down to Ground Zero and shot himself. ("That was *our* crazy guy," one of my friends lamented.) The next morning I woke up alone in a cold guest room in the same shitty world, made even more intolerable by the fact that I'd briefly believed it might not be inescapable.

No one stays secretly in love forever. My febrile infatuation broke, perhaps by no coincidence, a month after George's reelection. Lauren was in the middle of a humiliatingly public professional failure—"a fiasco," she kept calling it—while her husband was inconveniently out of the country. She called me at my cabin from New York one afternoon, disconsolate; she used the words *nervous breakdown*. I asked her: "Do you want me to come up there?" I told myself that I would've done the same thing for any good friend. I spent that evening with my arm around her while she sobbed in bars. Our waitress, assuming I was breaking up with her, quickly set our beers down in front of us and did not ask whether everything was all right. As we walked through the snowy streets that night, Lauren took my hand.

"Why do these conversations always have to happen at five a.m. when you're drunk and sleep-deprived?" I later asked my friend Gabe. He sagely explained: "Because that's when they happen."

I had rehearsed the Big Talk with Lauren, the confession of my love, countless times in my mind, recited it out loud like the St. Crispin's Day speech, but when the moment actually came I forgot all my lines and just sat there, choked and frozen. I'd always imagined it happening in some dream space, out of time, exempt from any consequences—some mountaintop, or the Bardo—but we were in Lauren's familiar kitchen, the next morning already starting to show in the sky. When she admitted that she might have fallen "a little bit in love" with me, I was unable to get my mouth to move, while inside I was yelling at myself. Once spoken aloud, made real, it might turn out to be a cheap, silly thing, easily busted. After a long, pained silence, I finally admitted that I felt the same way. "Except," I said, with difficulty, "not a little."

Readers who have been lured along this far by sexual tension may want their money back; nothing untoward happened between Lauren and me that night, or ever. We stayed up talking until dawn. She was flying across the country to join Lars early that morning, and she asked me if I would go with her to the airport. On the taxi ride she dozed with her head on my shoulder with the unselfconscious presumption of a little kid. The casual physical intimacy of it felt unreal. When I saw her off at the airport, I told her I loved her, and she did something like laugh, except sadly, and hugged me good-bye. Then I was alone, sleep-deprived, heartbroken and hungover, at LaGuardia.

Around seven a.m. I turned up looking haggard indeed on my friend Lucy's doorstep in Brooklyn, where I was granted asylum and fed blueberry oatmeal alongside her children. Later that morning—I like to imagine at the same moment—Lauren and I both threw up: I, bluely, in Lucy's bathroom, and Lauren in an airplane lavatory at thirty thousand feet, moving away from me at five hundred miles an hour.

The golden age of Athens lasted less than fifty years. America had about the same brief, dizzying time on top before we embarked on our own disastrous foreign expedition. Apparently hawks of the Vietnam era liked to cite Thucydides's *History of the Peloponnesian War* as a sort of code to identify themselves as clear-eyed practitioners of realpolitik as opposed to those pie-in-the-sky peaceniks. These people may not have read all the way to the end of the book, to the retreat from Syracuse, in which the invading Athenians are forced to flee on foot while their dying comrades beg them not to desert them, doomed to enslavement and slaughter. If they'd at least skimmed ahead or read the CliffsNotes, they might have been able to envision the unthinkable: ignominious defeat, a fiasco, the last helicopters lifting off the roof of the embassy, our former allies clinging desperately to the skids, dropping off one by one, abandoned.

When I first got involved with Lauren, I did not have an exit strategy. After any breakup, as after military defeats, there are always battling narratives, scuffles for the moral high ground, even if the difference in elevation is measured in inches. Lauren was angry at me for having kept my feelings for her secret for so long. I'd always thought I was being frankly sort of noble by keeping them to myself; all I could see was the damage it would do. I'd always assumed that what she didn't know couldn't affect her marriage. When I said this out loud, Lauren was too incredulous to be angry. "How could it not?" she said.

Lars was reportedly unfazed when Lauren confessed she'd gotten maybe a little inappropriately attached to me. "You're boy-crazy," he said. When I apologized to him over beers, he said, "I'm just sorry you kept yourself in such an unpleasant situation for so long." Lars was a practitioner of Zen Buddhism and disinclined to such things as punching. Or maybe he just trusted his wife—a trust that had proven, in the end, well justified.

"Are you *mad* at her, at all?" Lucy asked me, seeming very much to imply that maybe I should consider it. Lauren had probably been less oblivious to my devotion than she pretended, and doubtless she'd enjoyed being adored from anear. Who wouldn't? But we'd both known, on some level, what we were doing, and we both must've been getting something out of it for it to persist as long as it had. But I did think she was rewriting our history now, airbrushing out her own complicity. She told me over the phone that she couldn't help but reexamine our whole friendship in light of this revelation; it seemed to cover everything with an unwholesome glaze. I begged her not to say the word *glaze.* I pictured the gelatinous coating over a ham in a cookbook. She said it again, punitively—"*glllaaaaazzzze*"—leaning on it, giving the *l* a lot of thick, mucous palate and cruelly elongating the *z.*

Lucy's advice to me was to spend that winter with friends in Seattle instead of New York. I'd agreed this made sense, and yet, riding the train through North Dakota in January, staring out at that Siberian desolation, it was hard not to feel exiled. That was a bleak season; Bush's election in 2000 had been a coup or a fluke, but his reelection felt like a referendum on the war in Iraq, by then indisputably a disaster, and a majority of our fellow Americans had voted: more of the same. After that, a lot of liberals emotionally seceded, abandoning the nation to the will of the Shitheads. Our new official position on the war was: *Good luck with that. Let us know how that works out for you.* That winter I drew myself trying to cheer up the exiled Nixon on the beach at San Clemente, and lonely Pluto (also soon to be deposed) in love with the distant sun.

Falling out of love is like letting go of grief: a kind of betrayal. Lucy promised me that Lauren and I would get through this together and that our friendship would ultimately be stronger for it. "Just keep telling yourself, 'She is like a sister to me,'" she advised. I gave her a look like kids do when you tell them that someday they'll thank you for this. But what made it so painful was also what made it possible at all: it hadn't been just an infatuation. Lauren and I had begun as friends, not lovers going through the motions as a preliminary, and we were stubbornly determined to salvage that friendship. Over the next months we renegotiated its terms. Lauren imposed some conditions: some personal subjects were off-limits now; no unchaperoned visits, at least for a while; and no more code names. This last proscription hurt more than you might think. One of the things you lose when a relationship ends is the person you got to be in it.

In 2006, Lauren and Lars had a child (she'd revisited her "Fuck motherhood" policy) and moved back to the West Coast. Once in a while, on a visit, she and I would have a summit meeting to check in and see how we were each doing with "our whole, y'know, Thing." For a long time our friendship felt more intense and volatile than most, requiring active maintenance and tending, with little rifts and reconciliations. But over the years it slowly toughened, became less like some precious heirloom than a piece of luggage you've had since college—familiar and durable, unobtrusively beloved. I took it as a sign of recovery, a healthy overcorrection, when familiar foibles of Lauren's no longer seemed endearing and instead just got on my nerves. Eventually a day came when I got horribly heartbroken over someone else, and then Lauren got to hold me while I sobbed in public and everyone around us assumed she was breaking up with me. It was the first time since our big talk that I was grateful again to have this woman as a friend.

The fall of the Bush administration came in a way that, per history's usual MO, satisfied the demands of neither justice nor dramaturgy. Just a year after his reelection, George finally lost any credibility among all but that die-hard 35 percent of Americans who also believed in guardian angels, not because of the ongoing disaster abroad but because of a hurricane that gutted an American city. Katrina was an Iraq that happened at home, where reporters couldn't be embedded or the footage censored. Seeing their fellow countrymen's corpses floating in the streets, abandoned by a government that seemed to regard the Hobbesian social contract as some liberal boondoggle, Americans belatedly realized that the people running the country were a bunch of blustering fuckups who couldn't be trusted to cat-sit. On the day George had to announce that the economy had accidentally collapsed, I sketched his face from the TV screen, and I could see that he looked old and scared, and relieved to be on his way out.

The atmosphere on election night 2008 was ecstatic, aphrodisiac.

I watched the returns in an apartment full of friends in New York, but when the networks called the night for Obama, I rushed to call Lauren. I got the "circuits busy" signal for the first time since 9/11; everyone was calling everyone else, all across the country, a happy echo of that awful day at the other end of the decade. When I finally got through to her, Lauren said that the Bush years had gone on so long that we'd assumed this was just what the world was like: the shitheads would always win. We'd forgotten that it was only a phase, a passing spasm. We tried to imagine how people who'd lived their whole lives in the Soviet bloc, for whom that Potemkin empire had been the whole world, must've felt when the edifice of lies finally collapsed like a flimsy stage set and they found themselves, unimaginably, free.

Having spent years in love with a woman I knew I was never going to be with, protesting a war we knew we weren't going to stop, I do have to ask myself whether any of it was worth it. I know I should probably mourn the years I squandered loving someone else's wife, years I should've invested in building a history with someone that could endure. But I'm more often seized by regret that feels like panic when I realize that I wasted the prime of my creative life on political cartoons, an art form less enduring than bathroom graffiti and as critically esteemed as balloon animals. I sometimes used to hope the country would descend into fascism just so my cartoons would acquire some retroactive historical importance, like Grosz's art from the Weimar years. The last time I recalled aloud how frivolous and irresponsible it would've felt to draw cartoons about anything else in that time, Lauren commanded me: "Write that down! Write it down, with the date and time! I'm tired of reminding you." Maybe my relationship with Lauren—and it was a relationship, however lopsided and sexless—was, like my years as a political artist, unavoidable, something that had to be undergone. And I have to believe that that love, like that work, was not wasted. If I do ever end up in a lasting relationship with someone smart and sane and kind, it'll be because I first loved Lauren.

Or maybe that's just the sort of horseshit you have to tell yourself to get through the nights. Maybe love and patriotism are both adolescent illusions, scams to get us to have babies and kill strangers, and those irreplaceable years were simply lost to folly. We all idealize our lovers, but I was able to keep Lauren more pristine than most, since we never even kissed. That imaginary relationship also kept me conveniently unavailable for real ones. And all nations are imaginary—only the guns are real—but America is even more fictitious than most, held together less by any common ethnicity, history, or even ideology than by a myth. The "real" America, the one soldiers and protesters alike were fighting for, is always on the horizon, over the rainbow, the country seen from the mountaintop. Between conservatives' Rockwell nostalgia for an imaginary past and our own *Star Trek* vision of a dubious future, practically no one could even see the actual United States—just another dumb blundering empire, like Athens or Assyria or Austria-Hungary, that overextended itself and learned its limits too late.

I recently looked up that funeral director who'd left all those bodies out to rot in the woods. He served time in prison and had to write a letter of apology to the families of the dead, but he never gave any explanation for what he'd done—not to the families, the court, or reporters. "He probably doesn't have one that's very satisfying," Lauren wrote me. "Things just kind of got away from him." And after all, what conceivable explanation could make sense of such a thing? The bodies are still piling up, and we're all still declining to talk about it. The only honest reckoning of the war I ever heard was on a New York City sidewalk: one guy was grumbling about what a clusterfuck Iraq had become, and his friend said, "Yeah, but you were probably all for it at the time, just like I was." By the time the war formally ended, it was like hearing about the death of a celebrity I hadn't known was still alive.

I quit cartooning a few months after the inauguration in 2009, burned out on politics. George, in his retirement, took up painting. Recently he's been painting portraits of veterans wounded in his wars, like an act of penance. It's hard to remember now the passionate loathing I felt for this sweet, dithering doofus. Lauren thinks I was instinctively onto something in my characterization of him. I almost feel as if we might yet sit down together in some bar outside of time, where the casualties don't count, and say: *It was a crazy time, everybody got a little carried away, we were all just trying to do what we thought was right.** There wasn't a lot of winning for anyone that decade. All those base and vainglorious agendas collided to yield a vast disastrous trajectory no one had intended or desired—history as clusterfuck.

People started using the phrase *the new normal* whenever they saw soldiers loitering with submachine guns in subway stations, a sight formerly associated with military juntas, or had to remove their shoes and belts at the airport like prisoners on suicide watch—a nervous verbal shrug at the dystopian future we all now inhabited. We got used to ceding freedoms as matter-of-factly as we give out our credit card numbers online. Everyone assumed the government was monitoring our phone calls and emails, the same way we figure cell phones are giving us cancer. The police seemed less like public servants than a hostile army of occupation suppressing an insurgent population. School shootings went from freakish atrocities to something more like a teen fad. Torture became a common device in horror movies, spy thrillers, and police procedurals; rape and abuse were increasingly popular genres of porn. Even superheroes started killing the villains in their films. Young people don't say *the new normal* anymore; to them it's just normal. But I guess no one

* Though let's not descend to some false equivalency: our side was right and theirs was wrong. And we didn't get anyone killed.

finds themselves in the same country they were born in at the ends of their lives. We all die in exile.

Recently, during one of our long phone conversations, Lauren said she could now understand those aging boomers who still wax apoplectic about Nixon and Liddy. "They didn't know how *good* they had it with Nixon," she groused. She confessed she didn't know whether she'd ever be able to forgive the people of this country for how they'd acted after 9/11. I was talking to her from Bryant Park, behind the New York Public Library, where we'd once faced off against the NYPD. Like her, I'm still a largely unreconstructed American. Looking at the New Yorkers and tourists all around me—eating their lunches, consulting guidebooks, listening to headphones—I found it hard to unsee my compatriots as I'd seen them revealed in that crisis: as dumb, herdlike creatures driven by fear, clinging to the pant leg of Authority, happy to forfeit their birthright as citizens, willing to condemn thousands of strangers to death.

In retrospect, I don't believe anyone was really "misled" about Iraq; they were given acceptable excuses, like the consensual lies agreed upon by seducer and seduced. To me there's something almost optimistic about even the most cynical *realpolitik* explanations of the war, in that they all assume there's something rational and calculated behind these paroxysms of insane race hatred that periodically seize all tribes and nations. The phrase *War on Terror* seems nakedly telling now; the U.S. expended four trillion dollars, thousands of our countrymen's lives, and untold numbers of others' in a mass national effort to defeat a feeling. It was a mass human sacrifice to appease the god of death.

Lauren and I both worry that neither romantic nor political passion are renewable resources, and that with age we can deplete them. The news is starting to feel stale and predictable to me, like previews for remakes of movies that came out when I was in high school. At some point I realized that I hadn't told anyone I loved her since Lauren and I had our late-night talk over a decade before. A decade is not a recuperative period; it's what my life is like now, the new normal. When I didn't even vote in 2012, Lauren was too disappointed to lecture me. The morning after the election I contrived to go for several hours without finding out who'd won. This was, pretty obviously, not true indifference but the kind of studied inattention you cultivate toward something you can't bear to care about anymore, like contriving to be busy on your ex's wedding day.

"Not everybody loses that fire as they get older," said Lauren, "but I think most people do. It's the extraordinary ones who remain fighters for what they believe in till the end." So if we don't want to end up as '00s burnouts in 2047, boring the young with spittle-flecked rants about Donald Rumsfeld,* the question becomes: how to get past that godawful decade and its disillusionments? Lauren, ever the old-lady-in-training, said that the old people she admires, the ones we hope to be like ourselves one day, haven't lost their outrage but refined it into something finer, lighter, a precision instrument instead of a bludgeon. She pointed out that all our demonstrations against the Bush administration accomplished exactly nothing; her new slogan is: "No more grand gestures." It would mean finding a new kind of passion, one less idealistic and futile—messier, more real, arms deep in the shitwork of living instead of holding out for the impossible.

I hung up, as always, feeling saner. Lauren and I came through our own bout of irrational passion to a kind of love that's truer and more enduring. Over a decade later, Lucy's incantation has come true: Lauren is like a sister to me. Somehow we successfully navigated the transition from being friends to what you might call Platonic lovers to something we don't have a name for: exes who never dated, friends without benefits. We have fewer words in our

* If you don't know who this was, I have no wish to keep his name alive.

language to distinguish kinds of love than we do for distant cousins. I think now that what I mistook for romantic love was something rarer and more valuable, something I couldn't recognize for what it was. It was like thinking you've figured out a quick route to riches or lucked into another exotic backwater to conquer, never realizing that you've accidentally found America.

The Feast of Pain

Last week my friend Mishka and I, out of idle curiosity and a wistful nostalgia for a popular sedative of the 1970s that neither of us ever even got the opportunity to resist the temptation to take, conducted an Internet search for "do they still make 'ludes." Before we could finish typing the words *do they* the search engine autofilled: *still make quaaludes.* I felt a fond affinity for all depraved humanity.

This incident inspired me to enter various other open-ended interrogative phrases into the search engine to see what else it might autofill, as a sort of unscientific cross-sectional sampling of my fellow human beings' furtive curiosities and desires. Type in *why am I* and suggestions include: *so tired*

always cold
so ugly?

Why does produces: *salt melt ice*
my vagina itch
it snow?

Where is: my refund
Sochi
Chuck Norris?

Why can't: we be friends
I own a Canadian
I cry?

By the calendar, this long, dark, frigid winter—throughout which temperatures in the Northeast have ranged from cold to butt-cold, occasionally dipping down into what some climatologists classify as "butt-*ass* cold"—is over. Based on my conversations with everyone from close friends to Santo at the copy shop to total strangers on the subway, it seems as if these five months without light or exercise, all of us scrunching up our shoulders in pain whenever we step outside, holing up in bed and bingeing on Netflix, Jiffy Pop and booze, has left us all at the ends of our respective ropes. *Why does it snow?* Until by now, at the end of it, I find myself inappropriately cheered by glimpses of my fellow human beings' despair. My friend Kevin recently sent me an urgent text from a stall of the men's room at work:

I am pooping at work and there is some guy in here making loud grunting and loud pooping noises AND I THINK HE IS CRYING!

I was filled with a soaring joy.

This isn't exactly schadenfreude; it's something more complicated for which, as far as I know, there isn't a German compound, but if there were it'd be something like *Mitleidfreude*, compassion-joy—compassion in the literal sense of *suffering with*. It's the happiness, or at least the consolation, of knowing that things are tough all over. The other morning I heard the guy in the apartment next to mine utterly lose his shit: screaming obscenities, venting insane rage in the way that people only do when they're yelling at inanimate objects, a tone I know well. Shortly afterward he and I both left the building at the same time, and I saw him standing on the subway platform, to all appearances just another bored commuter waiting for the L train. I alone knew that five minutes earlier he had been out of his mind with psychotic rage. Then I realized that this might well be true of everyone else on the platform. It's heartening to know that everyone else is doing as badly as I am—all of us secretly screaming, pooping and weeping, googling *'ludes*.

I'm not just ghoulishly thriving off of others' pain; I'm happy to offer up my own, if it's any help. A friend of mine who lost her father a few weeks ago still lies awake at night sick with guilt, torturing herself by wondering what she should have done differently in his last hours. I ventured to confess, incommensurate though it was to her own grief, that I still wake up in the night panicking that I might've accidentally killed my cat with a flea fogger, even though the cat was nineteen years old and obviously moribund. To my relief, this delighted her. She still uses *flea fogger* as mental shorthand to keep from second-guessing herself into insanity.

Some people—quite a lot of them, evidently—are sustained by the Chicken Soup for the Soul book franchise, heartwarming anecdotes about acts of kindness and decency, forgiveness and redemption. (I am guessing; I've never opened one.) *De gustibus non est disputandum* and all, but, with respect to those who seek wisdom in the book bins of grocery stores, I require something more pungent than schmaltz in my own emotional diet. I never go to see any movie I suspect is a Triumph of the Human Spirit, either. Self-affirmation isn't nearly as validating for me as the frank acknowledgment that sometimes things just suck.

Not long ago I went to the East Village's Russian & Turkish Baths with my friend Jenny. People do not look their best coming out of the baths: their faces flushed and puffy, their hair damp and frazzled, any makeup they were wearing freshly boiled off, oils and toxins squozen out of their pores. Jenny looked at herself in the mirror in the women's changing room, made some half-assed effort at fixing herself up, then sighed resignedly. The girl next to her—who, it's worth mentioning, was much younger—reproached her in sororal solidarity: "No, you should never do that!" she told her. "We're *all* beautiful! You should say to yourself, 'I am beautiful!' " At the very moment my friend was telling me this story out in the foyer to the baths, a woman in her forties or fifties, passing by us, glanced at herself in the mirror and muttered: "Someone should just kill me." We were speechless with glee.

Earlier that same day I'd seen a guy have a heart attack in my doctor's waiting room. He hadn't even come in about his heart: he thought he just had the same lingering winter virus as the rest of us. He looked pretty bad—gray-faced and drenched in sweat—but I just figured, as he had, that he had the flu. But then he stood up unsteadily and told the receptionist: "Listen, I think I'm having a heart attack. Something's really wrong." She did not argue. They called 911 at once. I had to gather up the man's coat and bag for the EMTs to send along to the hospital. As I stood holding them, it was impressed upon me that this guy had not expected to go to the hospital today; this was just another errand on his to-do list before he went to work, as it was for me. As he was wheeled out of the office he was heard to moan: "Oh my God . . . This sucks . . . What the fuck?" Later that night, still a little in shock, I repeated these words to Jenny over Belgian ales. After a moment of solemn reflection, we both broke into shamefaced laughter. I swear we weren't laughing at him; we weren't gloating that it was him and not us.* It was that that

* When I called to get my own test results, I asked after the heart attack guy and was told he was fine—resting comfortably and expected to be out of the hospital in a couple of days. Although it occurs to me now that maybe that's just the official story they decided to give everyone, the way Dad used to tell us the dog had gone to live on a farm in Cecil County.

guy had spoken for all us suffering mortals, cursing feebly against the dying of the light. And we both knew, hearing this litany—*Oh my God, this sucks, what the fuck*—that when our own turns came to be wheeled away, neither of us was going to have anything more illuminating or dignified to say.

A friend of mine who, as a pastor, has access to a much more privileged vista of human suffering than I do recently told me she was tired of the phrase *first-world problems*—not just because it delegitimizes the perfectly real problems of those of us lucky enough to have adequate diets and Internet access, but because it denies the same ordinary human worries to people who don't. Are you not entitled to any existential angst or taedium vitae if you live in Chad? Must you always nobly suffer traditional third-world problems like warlords and malaria? It's true that when you're starving or scared for your children's lives, What It All Means is irrelevant; only once the basics are assured do you get to despair that there's just no point to anything because you will never ever get to go out with that girl on the subway or you put way too much parsley in the chicken soup and now it just tastes like parsley. These are the horrors you're spared if you're abducted into a child army.

But, if you're lucky, you graduate up the Maslovian pyramid to increasingly better problems, until eventually you get to confront the insoluble problem of being a person in the world. Even if we were someday to solve all our problems of economics and governance, people would still be unlucky in love, lonesome and bored, and lie awake worrying about the future and regretting stupid things they said in middle school. Utopia will still have forms to fill out, passive-aggressive bureaucrats, broken pipes and cavities, taxes, ads, assholes and bad weather. Time will pass without mercy. We will die. It will suck.

A couple of days ago I got dumped—first-world problem, I know. It's not as if it's a heart attack; it's just a rejection of your whole self by the person who knew you best. Our brief fake-out spring has been temporarily revoked, and it's raw and wet and cold out again, the wind maliciously splintering umbrellas, mocking our pitiful, spindly defenses. A friend of mine reports she saw people literally screaming today as the wind hit them in the streets, not in pain so much as an extremity of there-is-no-God rage and despair. The problem with breakup talks is that only one of you has rehearsed, or even has a script: the other one just sits there with his mouth open, trying not to cry, saying things like "So, wait—is this a breakup talk?" I'm still trying to reconstruct the conversation, stupidly trying to understand what was said to me, coming up with belated rebuttals. It's one of those days where you just have to force yourself through the motions, when the accumulated number of times you've had to make coffee and brush your teeth in your life seems too much to be borne, and doing the laundry is like cleaning out the Augean stables. You're like: *Someone should just kill me.* You sit on the edge of the bed for just one more minute, psyching yourself up to put on the other sock and commence yet another goddamned Tuesday, wondering: *Why can't I cry? Where is my refund? Do they still make 'ludes?*

The Dilemma

I'm starting this essay in medias res, hunkered down in a basement apartment—not exactly in hiding, more like lying low. Right across the plaza from me lives the woman I'm dating; one neighborhood away lives the other woman I'm dating. I'm currently on hiatus with both of them while they wait, with quickly diminishing patience, for me to choose between them.

As the cad in every bedroom farce says: I can explain. I'd been casually dating these two women for a few weeks—not an unheard-of or unethical practice, at least not in New York City, where people try on and discard partners like sunglasses in a drugstore. Inconveniently, they both seemed seriously interested in me, and, worse, I could find no good reason to break things off with either of them, which is not usually a problem for me. They were both smart, lovely, funny alpha girls who'd made interesting, unconventional lives for themselves in New York City. One was an author of YA fiction; she liked to tell anecdotes whose denouement was ". . . and then I won." When she'd told her friends that I was seeing someone else, they'd said, "He sounds like you." The other woman was intriguingly unlike me: a progressive pastor who'd started her own church in Brooklyn. She woke up in the morning and said things like "Today's going to be great." Meeting these women had been the first thing in a long time that had given me a glimmer of interest in the future.

After half a dozen dates with each of them, I began to get the uneasy feeling that it might soon be time to have a tentative little talk about exclusivity. It always seems like too soon to have this talk until suddenly it's too late. One day I saw both of them in the same afternoon, which was just a little too nerve-racking and sitcomish, and I realized this was no longer a tenable situation. So I decided to let each of them know, just as a courtesy, in the interest of full disclosure, that I was seeing someone else.

In retrospect, some critics have identified this as my mistake. One of the women involved has since explained that I should've said I was "seeing other people"; telling her I was seeing *one* other person made it too personal, inciting a spirit of competition. Each of them said that she appreciated my honesty but told me she couldn't continue seeing me as long as I was seeing someone else. They both insisted this was not an ultimatum and got very touchy if I called it one.

This ultimatum precipitated an unprecedentedly stressful month of my life known as the Dilemma. Having to choose one of these women to be, effectively, my girlfriend based on just a few dates reminded me of having to choose a college—the place where you're going to spend the next four years and figure out what you want to do with your life and make the kind of friends you'll later drive cross-country with—based on some glossy brochures and one visit. In fact I had to ask for an emergency twenty-four-hour extension to decide on a college, which is pretty much what I did in this case: asked each woman for a little time to clear my mind and think things over.

This has never once worked. Time to think things over has always resulted in exactly what's happening now: frenzied indecision, a manic paralysis, my brain revved up high in the red end of the tachometer, stuck in neutral. I lie awake thrashing wretchedly over the Dilemma every night; I groan aloud when I remember it on waking. Well-meaning friends try to help clarify my choice: Who's better in bed? Which of them has the better apartment? But it was no use: I wasn't seizing up because I wasn't sure which of them was the right choice, but because they were both right, and by choosing one I would forfeit the other.

One thing that makes decisions like this so paralyzing for me is that the immediate, concrete problem gets tangled up with the big abstract ones, which is a handy aptitude for an essayist but can make it hard to order in restaurants. Somehow the question of which woman to choose turned into the question of why we need to choose in the first place: who wrote up the boilerplate relationship contract, anyway, and why does it always include an ironclad monogamy clause? This world operates according to rules I was not around to vote on; marriage seems like one of those institutions that everybody agrees on but almost no one actually wants, like jobs, wars, or Christmas. In fact I'd always resented monogamy for the same reason I hate Christmas shopping: if something's obligatory, it isn't a gift.

"Maybe it's time for you to think about polyamory," suggested my ex-girlfriend T.J. I'd been shocked in ways that were hard to articulate when T.J., with whom I'd had a conventional, exclusive, boyfriend-girlfriend relationship years ago, had told me that she was now in an open relationship, with a primary partner and two regular long-term lovers, each of whom had their own girlfriends. For one thing, it profoundly fucked with my understanding of T.J., a fiercely cheerful, gamine girl you'd more likely imagine playing in a roller derby league. A large part of my reaction was sheer suppurating jealousy; I had to command her never again to speak to me of her boyfriend's burlesque-dancer girlfriend. Also I couldn't help but wonder how come this possibility had never come up back when she and I were dating.

Alongside the historic legal upheavals surrounding the expansion of the definition of marriage, a much quieter revolution seems to be taking place, extralegally and mostly under the media radar: a mass defection from traditional monogamy. Just as in Baltimore I'd always been at one remove from people who'd OD'd on heroin, in Brooklyn I was apparently only one degree of separation away from an underculture of people who were all companionably fucking each other. "They're mostly nerds," said T.J. "The kind of hipsters who knit." My friend Lorraine had told me there was a lot of overlap between the fetish community, the local contingent of Burning Man, and regulars at the Jazz Age party on Governors Island: they're people who like playing dress-up, reinventing themselves. In articles about polyamorists, their smug quotes reminded me of the naïve optimism of utopian communities; they were trying to erase history and rewrite human nature, like French revolutionaries starting the calendar over at the Year One.

The defenders of "traditional marriage," girding themselves to protect that sacrament against the sodomite horde, arrived about a half century late. The Pill may have been a more transformative invention than fossil fuels or nuclear weapons: as soon as people had access to sex without the threat of pregnancy, marriage became a vestigial custom, like shaking hands as a symbolic weapons check. When I was illegitimately conceived, only fifty years ago, my mother had to leave home under a cover story, and lived in an institution for young unwed mothers where mean ladies shamed them and boys followed them through the streets mocking them. Those mores now seem as archaic and cruel as child brides or foot-binding. Because I've never had any intention of having children, there's been no compelling practical reason for me to marry. And since at this point in the Malthusian curve, having children is about as responsible a decision as chucking your McDonald's wrappers onto the highway while blasting the AC with all the windows down, the whole get-married-have-kids-repeat pattern, the basic template for human life since day one, is suddenly just one option among many.

Too many, arguably. I've often thought that if I'd been impressed into an arranged marriage with one of my old girlfriends I'd've been perfectly happy—or at least no unhappier than most married people. I wished some village elder would choose one of the women in the Dilemma for me. Instead it was possible to squander my life in restless dissatisfaction, imagining there might still be some ideal person out there, tantalized by the illusion of bottomless choice, my relationships only ever provisional.

At the same time I was caught in my Dilemma, I got to watch an even more clichéd drama play out: a friend of mine left his wife for a younger woman. The first time Kevin told me, over the phone from a New Year's Eve party, that he was probably going to leave Renee, he sounded so laid-back and matter-of-fact about it that I wondered whether he might have a brain tumor. He and Renee had been together since we were all in our twenties; they were one of those couples whose names you said as a unit: *Kevin and Renee say hi.* He'd confessed to me a few months earlier that he had a huge crush on one of his coworkers. *Well, that happens*, I'd told him. *Don't let it wreck your life or anything.* He had immediately set about wrecking his life. He acted like a man with no choice in the matter. "I love the way she smells," he said.

I knew better than to try to argue with this kind of talk. I referred Kevin to a chapter called "The Pervert's Lament" from a chapter in *Sex at Dawn*, a then-popular book of speculative anthropology that purported to explain this very syndrome.* Men experi-

* Basically an extended appeal to nature, debunking the bias that monogamy is biologically determined and arguing that multiple partners, orgies, or gang rapes rather than pair-bonding were the norm in human prehistory. It's an attractively validating theory for the promiscuous, but the evidence is pretty inferential, plus the authors use words like *mighty* and *downright* as intensifiers.

ence the ebbing of testosterone in midlife as a creeping anhedonia: they don't enjoy the things they used to as much anymore; they wonder what the hell ever happened to them. One of the things that reliably boosts testosterone is a novel sexual partner, especially a younger one, which is why so many men feel restored to their true selves by such affairs after years of putting one foot in front of the other, and aren't content to keep mistresses on the side but instead abandon their families, trash their whole lives, and make themselves into buffoons out of *Der blaue Engel.* Kevin himself had nearly died of a heart attack a few years ago; he now took fistfuls of pills every day, and his heart was bristling with stents. The signature tag on his emails was: *Consider the finite time you will spend on Earth before closing this email.*

The two women in the Dilemma had put a moratorium on any actual dates but they were both still subtly conducting psyops campaigns. One of them sent me a Valentine's Day note. I covertly met the other for pie. The YA writer told me that she was sick of the clichéd device of romantic triangles in YA fiction; she just didn't buy it anymore. "If you really can't decide between two people," she said, in a way that seemed to contain some pointed subtextual message, "probably neither of those people is the right one for you." I thought this might just be something we all needed to tell ourselves to reassure ourselves that our choices are inevitable, preordained—hence people's blather about finding their one true unique soul mate in all the world, by astronomical coincidence, in their same homeroom/college class/tax bracket. I suspect the more unsettling truth is that there are quite a lot of people out there you could fall in love and spend your life with, if you let yourself.

The romantic ideal whereby the person you love, the person you have sex with, and the person you own property and have children with should all be the same person is a more recent invention than the telescope. In my own experience, love and lust have coincided about as often as looks and smarts, by happy coincidence. Lauren, one of my long-married friends, once advised me: "You don't need to get everything from your spouse" (though my friend Lucy added the sobering caveat: "You can't get breasts from your friends"). More than once I'd found my own romantic life split between someone with whom I felt genuinely intimate and someone to whom I was sexually addicted, like a typical Victorian hypocrite with his respectable Victorian wife and a bawdy Victorian whore. (And this distinction had less to do with any qualities intrinsic to those women than with the roles I projected onto them.)

It turns out this may not just be me. Sigmund Freud initially diagnosed the divorce between love and desire as a neurosis common among his male patients. He attributed it to unresolved incestuous wishes: we're attracted to people who unconsciously remind us of the first people we ever loved, for whom, unfortunately, sexual desire is taboo. So, although we feel most comfortable with people who feel like family and home, we're excited by people who are different, illicit, transgressive.* Domesticity dampens desire; it's just awkward to pack school lunches with someone the morning after they've seen you in the Nixon mask. Freud eventually came to regard it not as a neurosis to be cured but a more universal, irreconcilable tension, one of the hidden costs of civilization, the way that chronic back pain is a symptom of walking upright.

Freud's glum conclusion is to some extent corroborated by evidence that what he would've called "the affectionate and sensual"—what modern psychologists call attachment and sexuality—are

* One way to resolve this contradiction is through "optimal similarity," finding a mate in the Goldilocks zone: similar enough to feel safe, but different enough to be interesting. Which is one reason why, in much of the world, people marry distant cousins.

separate biochemical systems, with elevated levels of different chemicals associated with each. If you inject oxytocin into the brain of a ewe, she'll instantly bond with any lamb you put in front of her;* if you give testosterone to normally monogamous birds, they start sneaking around behind their bird wives' backs (and also Napoleonically expanding their territories).† In one of life's many humorous little double binds, these different chemicals tend to have an antagonistic effect on each other, meaning that love and lust can actively inhibit each other. Hence people feeling conflicted and guilty because they truly love their spouses but have no wish ever to sleep with them while secretly writhing with lust for some idiot.

Then again, this might not be the human condition, just the male one. Psychoanalyst Virginia Goldner disputes the consensus among her male colleagues that intimacy and desire are tragically incompatible, contesting that some people feel freer to express themselves sexually within the safety of a monogamous relationship. This echoes what some of my female friends have told me: that being in a relationship is liberating, allowing them to be more uninhibited with their partners and indulge in crushes and flirtations without any of the sticky complications of affairs.‡ Plus, Goldner points out, makeup sex.

---

* K. M. Kendrick, E. B. Keverne, B. A. Baldwin, "Intracerebroventricular Oxytocin Stimulates Maternal Behaviour in the Sheep." *Neuroendocrinology* 46, no. 1 (June 1987): 56–61.

† John C. Wingfield, "Androgens and Mating Systems: Testosterone-Induced Polygyny in Normally Monogamous Birds." *Auk* 101, no. 4 (Oct. 1984): 665–71.

‡ I don't want to descend to cheap men-versus-women generalizations here, but I will say that I don't often hear men talk about how much fun hitting on women can be but how tedious it is getting bogged down in all that fucking.

The way this evolutionarily jerry-rigged system is supposed to work is that sex lures you into a relationship long enough for an attachment bond to form (which, in adults, typically takes about two years), so that by the time the hormonal buzz wears off (which, conveniently, takes about three), you're bonded in a deeper, more enduring way and will then be willing spend the next twenty years together in indentured drudgery: managing tantrums, wiping up mucus and sputum, and paying for Pokémon, karate, and college. As many have noted, this system is imperfect in practice. But nature did not invent this system to make us happy; it invented it to make more people.

T.J., in the honeymoon phase of her open relationship, felt like she'd successfully cut through the whole psychosexual Gordian knot. She proselytized about polyamory, pointing out how our whole society—tax codes, legal and medical rights, social welfare programs—is biased in favor of long-term, monogamous relationships. (The most outspoken proponents of polyamory I've known have all been women, perhaps because they have more social taboos to overcome; a polyamorous man is just an opportunistic sleaze per everyone's expectations, but a poly woman is treated more like a traitor to her gender.) Like my YA author girlfriend, she'd lost all patience for plots that turned on temptation, jealousy, or infidelity, the same way she got exasperated by Dostoyevsky's compulsive gamblers. Her solution was: *Why not fuck them both?* She'd watched her boyfriend have sex with his ex-girlfriend, she told me, and it hadn't bothered her at all. I found myself dwelling unhealthily on this mental image, although I couldn't tell whether it aroused me or crept me out.

T.J. assuaged my envy by advising me that although polyamory multiplies the amount of sex you have, it exponentiates the number of relationship talks you have to have. During the Dilemma, around Valentine's Day—an occasion everyone agrees is a meaningless greeting-card holiday but which seems to trigger the same sorts of histrionic crises as weddings and funerals—I had to have six relationship talks in the space of two weeks, which is more than I normally like to have in a year. When I heard that some poly people bought Christmas gifts not only for their various partners but for their *partners'* partners, I decided: *Forget it—I'm out.*

During the Dilemma, Kevin came to visit me in New York in the middle of what he was calling a "trial separation" from Renee. I had just gotten an alarming late-night phone call from Renee, who'd taken every sedative in the house in an effort to fall asleep, and felt it incumbent on me to give him a little talking-to. "Renee sat next to your bed every day for a month when you were in the hospital," I reminded him. "She's put up with a lot from you. Even if you leave her," I said, "you owe it to her to treat her with respect and salvage some sort of relationship with her." I relayed a piece of old-world wisdom a friend had been given by a Haitian cabdriver: *Your mistress must respect your wife.*

My stern message might've gotten lost in the noise of mixed signals, since we also misbehaved like drunken twenty-two-year-olds the way we do every time we see each other. We met some German girls at a barbecue place and ended up spending the whole night with them, eating thick glistening slabs of pork belly, drinking pints of beer, smoking pot back at their hostel, and dancing to '80s music in a nautically themed bar. Although nothing actually Happened with these girls, I reflected, hungover in bed the next day while begging Kevin to stop talking for just one minute and please put on some pants, that it's the lure and pursuit of sex that keeps life interesting. On a spring day in New York City, the nonstop parade of the excruciatingly beautiful and heartrendingly hot makes the city seem like a bottomless cornucopia of erotic opportunity. Like many men, I am tormented by the delusion that for every attractive woman I see there is some hypothetical sequence of events that will lead to me having sex with her, and end up damning myself as a coward and a failure the 99.9999907 percent of the times this fails to happen.

Except how many times have I ever actually gone to a party or a bar and ended up getting the number of/making out with/going home with someone I met there? Even on the rare occasions when this has happened, there have been moments when it's occurred to me that it's three a.m., and I'm tired, and this is all getting to be rather a lot of work, and in truth I might've been happier watching a movie with the cat on my lap. It's the tantalizing *possibility* of sex—reinforced, like an addiction to nickel slots, by the rare, sporadic payoff—that gives life its luster.

The closest I'd ever come to infiltrating the polyamorous lifestyle was when my friend Lorraine had invited me to a "kissing party," which proved to be an adult game of spin-the-bottle. I felt I went home a winner: kissing a whole roomful of pretty girls was exactly as fun I'd imagined it would be—a warm, light-headed hormonal high I could feel for hours afterward, like an opiate—and I did not have to kiss the fat guy in the wizard hat. But I also found that, with the barrier of having to *convince* pretty girls to kiss you miraculously lifted, some of its allure is diminished. Without the possibility of rejection, kissing is almost as worthless as self-publishing. Freud again: "It can easily be shown that the psychical value of erotic needs is reduced as soon as their satisfaction becomes easy." Also some people are terrible kissers.

What might be hardest to give up for the sake of monogamy isn't sleeping around so much as a certain self-image that goes with it: I liked thinking of myself as single—available, interesting, faintly dangerous. Undomesticated. So many couples seem inert, done, the men tamed and denatured, the women wearing those brittle middle-age helmets of hair, blunt as a cab's OFF DUTY light. I once asked a writer I admired, whom I'd noticed was drinking soda water in a bar, whether he drank. "I'm spiritually a drinker," he said. "I no longer practice." It sounded like a well-rehearsed answer. He'd found a way of maintaining his street cred as a Drinker—rowdy, irreverent, and fun-loving—while forgoing the behavior that defined that identity. I wondered whether it was possible to do something similar with monogamy—to remain spiritually single without sleeping around.

My friend Lauren told me that back when she was young and single there was a certain kind of guy she'd never liked because they only ever seemed to be provisionally present—always keeping their coats on, sitting on the arm of the sofa, affecting an air of being just about to take off for a better party somewhere else. Later, she said, after everyone got married and had children, those same guys were exactly the same, except that now their excuse was that they had to get home to the wife and kids—sorry, you know how it is. Both roles, Party Guy and Family Man, were just different excuses for being withholding, not quite there—unavailable. The guys she's always liked have a way of letting you know that you have their full attention, of being flirty and confiding and genuinely engaged, even if you both know nothing's going to come of it. They are available in a way that has nothing to do with cheating. Lauren herself is happily married and an incorrigible flirt. "My head is easily turned," she sighs.

Kevin moved in with his new girlfriend four months after I'd first learned of any serious trouble in his marriage. Even his friends were discomfited by the abruptness of it, like citizens waking up to news of an overnight coup. He sent me a text:

> I have to say this midlife crisis thing has been excellent. I have behaved selfishly and it has been fantastic. I am happy as fuck.

Kevin has a signature move when he's stuck in traffic: just driving up the shoulder for as far as a mile to get to the next exit, an unapologetic fuck-you to the whole highway social contract. It had become an eponym among his friends: "Should we Kevin it?" This maneuver outrages his fellow motorists, all dutifully suffering through rush hour. He'd also become a pariah among his former friends and coworkers since leaving Renee, even though both of them seemed happier now than when they'd been married. (Renee had begun running, returned to her premarital weight, and was dating again.) His offense wasn't just disloyalty or callousness but flouting the social order; it scared them the way the death of someone their own age does, reminding them that their own marriages might not be as placid or stable as they seemed. Maybe this is also why so many monogamists find polyamory, open marriage, and other defections from fidelity so obscurely threatening, something to be frowned on or quashed, in the same way that capitalism has to buy out or carpet-bomb any alternative economic system, no matter how penny ante or out of the way it may be.

The real currency of affection in T.J.'s open relationship turned out to be not sex but time. Her boyfriend would never commit to an evening out with T.J. and her friends ahead of time because he might have some work to do: his standard RSVP was "Can we play it by ear?" She hadn't minded watching him fuck his ex, but when she found out he was cooking dinner for one of his other girlfriends—something he never seemed to have time to do for her—she was furious. "And then *she stood him up* and *I ate it*," she told me, smoldering with pyrrhic triumph. "That must have been a bitter dinner," I ventured. By way of reply she stared unblinkingly at me and pantomimed chewing forkful after forkful of food, slow and purposeful as a cobra.

She made every effort to instruct her boyfriend in how to keep her, issuing an explicit list of things he could do to let her know that she was loved. One item on the list was: *Make pancakes for me.* He had never once done this. And he *still* didn't do it, even after receiving the list. I'm sure he intended to make pancakes some Sunday morning soon, but it was never the right Sunday, there was always something else he had to do, and somehow he never got around to it. When she finally informed him that she'd made arrangements to move out, then, oh yes, then came the frantic belated making of pancakes, many, many of them, but alas, T.J. had made up her mind. The pancakes came too late.

Let traditionalists take pause before seizing vindication from this story. The failure of T.J.'s open relationship doesn't prove that polyamory doesn't work any more than the failure of Kevin's marriage means that monogamy doesn't. Maybe the moral is, nothing works. How could any single system hope to regulate the mating behavior of an animal afflicted with consciousness? Psychoanalyst Irwin Hirsch suggests, in a tone that sounds a lot like resignation, that the ideal of a long-term monogamous relationship that successfully integrates love and sex might ultimately be doing more harm than good, presuming that monogamy is a priori a virtue and requiring everyone to conform to a narrow, if not imaginary, norm.* It's not as if psychoanalysts' own relationships are all models of happy functionality, he admits.

"Psychoanalytic research . . . is quite satisfied if reforms make use of its findings to replace what is injurious by something more advantageous," Freud wrote, "but it cannot predict whether other institutions may not result in other, and perhaps graver, sacrifices." It's probably just as well that Freud didn't live long enough to know about *Playboy* and the Pill, free love and key parties, bukkake and dogging. Whether the sexual revolution has brought about a net increase or decrease in human happiness would be hard to gauge. Traditional solutions to the problem of monogamy were rigid and

---

* Irwin Hirsch, PhD, "Imperfect Love, Imperfect Lives: Making Love, Making Sex, Making Moral Judgments." *Studies in Gender and Sexuality* 8, no. 4 (2007): 355–71.

institutional, involving systemic incentives and penalties like tax breaks, dowries, and stoning, but since the chain-reaction fission of the nuclear family, they're increasingly improvised ad hoc. I know married couples who've had consensual flings or foursomes, some who maintain a French don't-ask-don't-tell policy, and one who observe what they call "the Week of Decadence," an annual sanctioned holiday from fidelity. One woman told me she'd married her best lover instead of her best friend, figuring she could always work on the friendship; a male friend confided that he and his wife like to keep a certain playful distance, making a game of whether he can win her over. We all assume we're talking about the same things when we use words like *marriage* or *relationship*, but I suspect that beneath these labels, however normal or similar they may look from the outside, people's private lives are as different from one another as frigid Neptune is from lead-melting Venus beneath their bland blankets of cloud.

"Making decisions takes no time," writes Lionel Shriver. "It's the not deciding that takes so much time." Per my usual MO, I put off the moment of decision in the Dilemma until the deadline, when both women were literally minutes from breaking up with me, inflicting the maximum possible suffering on everyone involved, including myself. But in the end I made my choice. Like most big decisions, it looks inevitable in retrospect: it was the pastor's infectious happiness, her conviction that *today was going to be great*, that won me over. She made happiness seem like no big deal, a thing you could manage to pull off every day, instead of the distant, mythical goal it had always seemed to me, something more like world peace. I would never regret the choice I'd made, though I'd always regret the one I hadn't.

I had hoped that having made a choice in the Dilemma would at least put an end to my month of nerve-racking tension, but instead I found myself still secretly panicked. Had I just somehow cornered myself into committing to an exclusive relationship with someone I hadn't even slept with yet? This did not sound like me; in fact it sounded insane, like an arranged marriage in which the bride is veiled up till the last second. Monogamy still felt like something being imposed on me, not my choice, but I couldn't figure out how to negotiate a compromise. It didn't seem like the sort of thing you could ease into gradually; apparently backsliding was a big deal. In retrospect, it's obvious that my irrational sense that I'd somehow been entrapped into this relationship was a symptom of my fear that it was a serious one. My trepidation was both justifiable and stupid. Of course no one is the Right Person when you meet her; this is just an illusion necessary to lure you into investing the years and making the sacrifices necessary to love someone. It's like telling yourself your book is going to be a masterpiece and make you rich in order to undertake the laborious ordeal of writing it. It's only after making all those compromises and forfeitures, and amassing a shared fortune in memories, regrets, in-jokes and secrets, fights and reconciliations, that that person becomes the only possible one for you, unique and irreplaceable.

T.J. changed her answer in the "What I'm Looking For" category on her dating profile from "anything goes" to "monogamous relationship/marriage." Almost immediately, after a string of emotionally absent boyfriends, she found a guy who unabashedly adored her; when she excused herself to get a drink at a party he would talk behind her back about how amazing she was. Within a year of their meeting, they'd moved in together, she'd proposed to him, and she was pregnant.

Kevin is already married to his new girlfriend. She forged her own wedding ring out of a gold Krugerrand he'd given her, and makes her own marmalade from things like Meyer lemons and quince. They sent me a few jars in the mail. Kevin tells me he's had to renounce getting pissed off in traffic or snapping at panhandlers, because he feels he's used up his lifetime quota of Asshole Points. He recently sent me a photo of a tombstone he likes to sit beside when he eats his lunch, a massive boulder engraved, by coincidence, with his own last name. "I love that fucking rock," he wrote. When people ask me what I think about Kevin's divorce and remarriage, all I can tell them is: It's really good marmalade.

Not long after I'd made my decision in the Dilemma, my friend Lucy invited me to a swanky literary event. There were a lot of young women there—interns, assistant editors, agents, publicists, aspiring writers—all wearing sexy party dresses. This was also one of the few imaginable venues in which my own meager stock, being A Writer, might conceivably have any value. But I wasn't going to be flirting or asking out or going home with anybody there. You become an artist in the hope of attracting girls; now that I had a girlfriend, why was I an artist? Come to think of it, now that I was in a relationship, what was the point of social functions—of dress-up events, clubs or concerts, parties or bars, of ever going out at all? Why was I here: to talk with other writers? There is nothing writers loathe more. To *network*? Jesus—please.

Later the lights went down, the music got loud, and the women all started to dance while I sank into a bitter self-pitying funk. For reasons as yet unexplained by evolutionary psychology, almost all women love to dance. They also like to pressure men to dance, despite our repeated protests that we really don't want to, no, seriously, because they know that once we're out there, we will love it. It's supposed to be cute and fun, their cajoling you out onto the floor as if onto a gangplank, forcing you to jiggle and twitch miserably in front of everybody. I wondered whether it was some kind of test or ordeal ritual for potential mates, like working for months in order to purchase a single token stone. Also, my dancing has been likened to the flailing of those inflatable tube-men who advertise used car lots, and I was afraid I would be mocked.

But then the DJ played "I Want You Back" by the Jackson 5. That first ecstatic moan from the throat of Motown's own castrato, voluptuous and pure as the sinuous clarinet that opens Debussy's *Prelude to the Afternoon of a Faun*—who can resist it? Lucy's a married woman, with two kids; she and I have never dated or slept together or even so much as drunkenly made out on a New Year's Eve. But I've known her since she was thirteen, a quiet, awkward adolescent with a secret crush on me, long before she became the formidable person she is now. She has held me while I've cried; she sometimes appears in my dreams, taking charge and hailing cabs. We are intimates. Maybe this is what Lauren meant by being available without having to give everything away. It's not unlike dancing—a ritualized pantomime, all bold approach and coy demurral, but not necessarily an invitation or prelude; it can be a pleasure in itself. Maybe it's all less a matter of the right person, or the right time, than of waiting for the right song to come on. I held out my hand to Lucy, which she took with delighted surprise, and we stepped out onto the floor.

A Man and His Cat

"That cat makes *no positive contribution* to this household!"

—Dad, denouncing our family cat, Mow

I have lived with the same cat for the last nineteen years—by far the longest relationship of my adult life. Under common law, this cat is my wife. I fall asleep at night with the warm pleasant weight of the cat on my chest. The first thing I see on most mornings is the foreshortened paw of the cat retreating slowly from my face and her baleful crescent glare informing me that it is Cat Food Time. As I often tell her, in a mellow, resonant Barry White voice: "There is no *luuve* . . . like the *luuve* that exists . . . between a man . . . and his cat."

The cat is jealous of my attentions; she likes to sit on whatever I am reading, walk back and forth and back and forth and back and forth in front of my laptop's screen while I'm working, and unsubtly interpolate herself between me and any woman I may happen to have over. She and my ex-girlfriend Kati Jo, who was temperamentally not dissimilar to the cat, instantly sized each other up as enemies, a couple of rival females after the same eligible bachelor. (I remember Kati Jo saying, with rueful respect, after the cat had successfully feigned affection as a ruse to get her claws into Kati's cashmere sweater: "You win, you bitch.") When I am physically intimate with a woman, the cat does not discreetly absent herself but sits on the edge of the bed facing rather pointedly away from the scene of the debauch, quietly exuding disapproval like your grandmother's ghost.

I realize that people who talk at length about their pets are tedious at best, and often pitiful or repulsive. They post photos of their pets online, speak to them in disturbing falsettos, dress them in elaborate costumes, carry them around in handbags and BabyBjörns, and have professional photographs of them retouched to look like old master oil portraits. When people over the age of ten invite you to a cat birthday party or a funeral for a dog, you need to execute a very deft maneuver, the etiquette equivalent of an Immelmann turn, to decline without acknowledging that they are, at least in this one area, insane.

This is especially true of childless people like myself, who tend to become emotionally overinvested in their animals and dote upon them in a way that gives onlookers the willies. Often the pet seems to be a focus or joint project for a relationship that's lost any other raison d'être, like rehabbing a house or becoming insufferable foodies or getting heavily into cosplay. Or having children. When such couples finally have a human child, their cats or dogs must be bewildered to find themselves unceremoniously demoted to the status of Pet; instead of licking the dinner plates clean and piling into bed with Mommy and Daddy, they're given bowls of actual dog food and tied to a metal stake in a circle of dirt.

I looked up how much Americans spend on pets annually and have concluded that you do not want to know. I suppose I could tell you what I spend on my own cat's special kidney-health cat food and kidney and thyroid medications, plus periodic blood tests that always cost $300 and come back normal, but I have never even calculated what this amounts to per year, lest I be forced to confront some uncomfortable facts about me. The implication of our mass national spending on luxury products to pamper animals who seem happiest while rolling in feces or eating the guts out of rodents—who don't, in fact, seem significantly less happy if they lose half their limbs—is probably also something we don't want to think about. Something so obvious it hardly needs pointing out about the epidemic loneliness of a society in which people live across the country from their families, don't know their neighbors, fuck strangers, and see their friends mostly online.

I suspect that people have a certain reservoir of affection that they need to express, and in the absence of any more appropriate object—a child or a lover, a parent or a friend—they will lavish that same devotion on a pug or a Manx or a cockatiel, even on something neurologically incapable of reciprocating that emotion, like a monitor lizard or a day trader or an aloe plant. As usual, someone else turns out to have preempted this insight a couple of thousand years before I was born; in his essay "How the Soul Vents Its Emotions on False Objects When True Ones Are Lacking," Montaigne cites Plutarch as speculating, in regard to those who form attachments to monkeys and small dogs, that "the affectionate part of us, in this way, for lack of a legitimate object, fashions a false and frivolous one rather than remain useless." Konrad Lorenz corroborates this theory in *On Aggression*, describing how, in the absence of the appropriate triggering stimulus for an instinct, the threshold of stimulus for that instinct is gradually lowered: a male ring dove deprived of female doves will attempt to initiate mating with a stuffed pigeon, a rolled-up cloth, any vaguely bird-shaped object—eventually even with an empty corner of its cage.

You don't need to turn to the animal world for an illustration of this principle; this city around me, supposedly teeming with erotic possibility, is full of people alone in their apartments stimulating themselves to orgasm to 300dpi-resolution images of human beings copulating on screens. Our obscene spending on pets may be symptomatic of the same chronic deprivation as are the billion-dollar industries in romcoms and porn. Someone who taught ESL once told me that her foreign students were bewildered by Americans' sentimental attachment to their pets. She thought it must have something to do with unconditional love; my own belief is that Americans are so starved for any kind of connection that they would fall in love with a bug if it's all they could afford. This is the country that invented the Pet Rock.

Although I can see this syndrome as pathological in others, I myself am its textbook illustration, the Elephant Man of the condition. I do not post photographs of my cat online and try not to talk about her to people who couldn't be expected to care, but at home, alone with the cat, I behave like some sort of deranged archfop. I have made up dozens of nonsensical names for the cat over the years—the Quetzal, Quetzal Marie, Mrs. Quetzal Marie the Cat, the Inquetzulous Q'ang Marie—even though as far as I can tell the only word in her listening vocabulary is *cat*. There is a litany I recite aloud to her every morning, a sort of daily exhortation that begins: "Who knows, Miss Cat, what fantastickal adventures the two of us will have to-day?" I have a song I sing to her when I'm about to vacuum, a big, brassy Vegas showstopper called "That Thing You Hate (Is Happening Again)." We have been kicked off a train together and marooned in Wilmington, Delaware. We collaborate on compositions on my foot-pedal pump organ, like the Hideous Cat Music, in which she walks back and forth at her discretion on the keyboard while I work the pedals. The Hideous Cat Music resembles the work of Hungarian composer György Ligeti, with extended aleatory passages and unnervingly sustained tone clusters. I have as many little routines and peeves, in-jokes and stories with this animal as I've had in years-long relationships.

I never meant to become this person. The cat turned up as a stray at my cabin on the Chesapeake Bay when I was sitting out on the deck eating leftover crabs. She was only a couple of months old then, small enough that my friend Kevin could fit her whole head in his mouth. She appeared from underneath the porch, piteously mewling, and I gave her some cold white leftover crabmeat. I did not know then that feeding a stray cat is effectively adopting that cat. For a few weeks I was in denial about having a cat. My life at that time was not structured to accommodate the responsibility of returning home once every twenty-four hours to feed an animal. I posted flyers in the post office and grocery store with a drawing of the cat, hoping its owner would reclaim it. It seems significant in retrospect that I never entertained the possibility of taking the cat to the pound. When I left for a long weekend to go to a wedding in another state, my friend Gabe explained to me that the cat clearly belonged to me now. I protested: this was a strictly temporary situation until I could locate a new home for the cat, I explained; I was not going to turn into some Cat Guy.

"How would you feel," he asked me, "if you were to get home from this weekend and that cat was gone?"

I moaned and writhed in the passenger seat.

"You're Cat Guy," he said.

It's amusing now to remember the strict limits I originally intended to place on the cat. I was not going to be one of those indulgent, doting Cat Guys who lets a pet control his life. Not I. One of the boundaries I meant to set was that the cat would not be allowed upstairs, where I slept. Now I am wounded when the cat declines to sleep with me and wonder why she is being so standoffish.

"You're in *love* with that cat!" my ex-girlfriend Margot once accused me. To be fair, she is a very attractive cat. I've told the cat that people talk about it. One friend described her as a "supermodel cat," with green eyes dramatically outlined in what he called "cat mascara" and bright pink nose leather (a phrase I learned at a cat show, describing the finely pebbled texture of the skin on a cat's nose). Her fur, even at age nineteen, when a lot of cats' hair gets matted and dull, is still soft and pleasant to touch. It is just about impossible, when I see her curled up asleep on the couch with her head upside down, not to bury my whole face directly in the center of the warm plush cat ball and say *O mu mu mu mu mu.*

An artist I dated drew a cartoon pamphlet called *The Bachelor Cat*, illustrating a specific type she'd repeatedly encountered. This isn't an easy thing to come out of the closet about; there is a certain stigma attached to Cat Bachelorhood. A friend once wrote a ribald and libelous poem about my cat and me, whose first line was *Tim is a catfucker*. When I was looking for a rideshare for my cat and myself on Craigslist, one respondent slipped it matter-of-factly into the middle of a paragraph about logistics that he'd be willing to take care of gas and tolls in exchange for "a little road head once we hit the turnpike." When I politely declined, he wrote back: "What's the problem? You're a single dude with a cat. Am I missing something?" For a brief weird period of my life a TV production company expressed an interest in creating a reality show about my cat and me for Animal Planet.* My friend T.J. proposed the obvious title for this show: *Pussywhipped!*

It might be relevant to mention here that I have never so much as cohabited with a human female. It has to be admitted that loving a cat is a lot less complicated than loving a human being, if only because animals can't ruin our fantasies about them by talking. (I should note that most of my little routines and in-jokes with the cat, except for the hideous cat music, are one-sided.) Although of course there's a good deal of willful ignorance, projection, and self-delusion involved in loving other human beings, too. Even though we can talk to each other, argue, and explain ourselves, we can't

---

* The network was looking for a new show about someone who worked with animals for a living, but they'd already played out the obvious professions—vets, dog trainers, lion tamers. A production company had been developing a show around a psychic who received her psychic vibrations via the medium of her cat, except that then the psychic, in an evidently unforeseen development, died. Disquietingly, her cat died *a week before she did*, which seemed like some sort of posthumous validation of her, or at least the cat's, paranormal powers.

know each other from the inside. It requires an effort of empathy and imagination to catch some glimpse of the human being in front of us through the interference of our own desires: distorted reflections of our own families, exes, girls we had crushes on in grade school, and dumb ideas gleaned from movies and pop songs. In Carson McCullers's short story "A Tree • A Rock • A Cloud," a drifter in a café explains to a boy that he has made a study, a discipline, of love and is working his way up toward being able to love another person by first learning to love little things—a goldfish, or a face in a crowd. Loving a woman, he says, is "the most dangerous and sacred experience in God's earth," the thing we should train all our lives for instead of blundering into it as clueless boys.

But then who's to say what is or isn't an "appropriate" object of affection? The desire to connect is fundamentally healthy, even if its expression is misdirected. Devotion is no less heartfelt when its object is absurdly incommensurate to it. I'm not going to validate social conservatives' slippery-slope warnings by making a plea for legalized man-cat marriage here, but I will maintain that my relationship with this animal is not wholly unilateral or imaginary; there is some reciprocity to it. It is not like keeping the TV on all day or being best friends with Jesus; someone else is there. That cat doesn't know my name, couldn't even understand the concept of names, but in some ways she knows me better than some women I've dated. In the '60s it was speculated that cats might possess some sort of extrasensory perception, and although I'm officially a skeptic on the subject of cat ESP, I can understand how people could entertain the idea, so uncanny is my own cat's ability to interpret and anticipate my behavior. She dreads being confined to the hated travel box and has come to associate any major housecleaning with an imminent move, so that now, when she notices me getting serious about tidying up, she instantly makes herself unavailable, hiding under the bed or behind the couch in a way that I feel demeans us both.

The cat has also efficiently conditioned my behavior. Biologists call cats "exploitive captives," an evocative phrase that might be used to describe a lot of relationships, not all of them interspecies. I made the mistake, early on, of feeding the cat first thing in the morning, forgetting that the cat could control when I woke up—by meowing politely, sitting on my chest and staring at me, nudging me insistently with her face, or placing a single claw on my lip. She refuses to drink water from a bowl, coveting what she believes is the higher-quality water I drink from a glass. I have attempted to demonstrate to the cat that the water we drink is the very same water by pouring it from my glass into her bowl right in front of her, but the cat was utterly unmoved, like a Birther being shown Obama's long-form birth certificate. In the end I gave in and now serve her water in a glass tumbler, which she has to stick her whole face into to drink from. What the cat would like best would be for me to sit without moving with her on my lap forever, and I have often pled inability to come to the phone or make dinner because the cat is asleep on my lap and there is nothing to be done. She registers her protest at my extended absences by pissing on my things, leaving neat little cat turds on my bed like ominously terse notes from your spouse, or, most recently, by starting to die whenever I try to leave town.

Last year she was diagnosed with kidney failure, an affliction common to aging cats, and given only a year or two to live. Recently I left the cat in the care of my mother while I went on a cross-country trip for the holidays. When I called to check in, my mother told me that the cat had stopped eating. Mom, a former nurse, described her as "febrile." A vet prescribed an antibiotic and an appetite stimulant. I called home daily for the cat report. For a while the cat seemed to rally, but then Mom told me she'd stopped eating again and said she "couldn't vouch for the cat's condition" on my return. I weighed the insanity of flying home early against the lifelong remorse of letting the cat die while I was on vacation, and in the end I spent an appalling amount of money on a last-minute, first-class transcontinental ticket the day before Christmas Eve.*

To spare you the suspense I suffered, I'll just skip to the dénouement: *fucking cat fine.* So now I am effectively held hostage by a cat, unable to travel for any lengthy period lest she expire to punish me. I know from growing up on a farm that cats prefer to die by themselves, and have heard that house cats often die while their owners are away. So I'm trying to tell myself that if the cat does die on me while I'm out of town, it won't be because she pined tragically away for me or died to spite me but because my absence gave her a window of opportunity to die in peace, unmolested by my love.

Whenever I feel guilty about abandoning the cat with a friend for a few days or weeks, or dragging her from sublet to sublet like Céline carrying the long-suffering Bébert through the entire Second World War, or keeping her locked in a New York City apartment all winter like some cruel Bluebeard imprisoning his bride in a turret—whenever, in other words, I feel embarrassed about factoring a house pet's desires into major life decisions—some grown-up-sounding part of me tells myself: *It's just a cat.* Legally, the cat is my possession, even if she acts more like a high-maintenance girlfriend. Some vestige of the Cartesian belief in animals as objects persists in our society—mostly, I suspect, because it's convenient, since we still need to use them as experimental subjects or clothing and really like how some of them taste. (I discussed all this with a friend of mine while dining on the muscles ventral to the lumbar vertebrae of a pig, an animal far more intelligent than my cat, in a honey-Dijon glaze.) It's assumed that animals lack what we call

* It occurred to me only later that maybe the cat was not the one who was exaggerating her declining health to get me back home for Christmas.

consciousness, although no one can define what exactly this is, and how we can pretend to any certainty about an animal's subjective mental experience has never been made clear to me. To anyone who has spent time with an animal, the notion that they have no interior lives seems so counterintuitive, such an obdurate denial of the empathetically self-evident, as to be almost psychotic. I suspect that some of these same psychological mechanisms must have allowed people to rationalize owning other people. Anyone in the antebellum South who'd considered wrecking his own livelihood out of some crackpot notion of equality might have been accused of anthropomorphizing.

Another part of me, perhaps more sentimental but also more truthful, has to acknowledge that although this cat may be less complex than me, perhaps not what we'd call self-aware, she is still undeniably another being in the world, a fellow Self experiencing her one chance at being alive, just like I am. It's always amused me to hit or elongate the word *you* in speaking to the cat, as in "*Yooouu* would probably *like* that!"—because it's funny (and funny often means disquieting and true) to remind myself that there really is another ego in the room with me, with her own likes and dislikes and idiosyncrasies and exasperatingly wrongheaded notions. It is not an insoluble epistemological mystery to divine what the cat wants when I wake up and see her face two inches from mine and the Tentative Paw slowly withdrawing from my lip.

Sometimes it strikes me that *an animal is living in my house*, and it seems as surreal as if I had a raccoon or a kinkajou loose in here. There are plenty of opportunities for misinterpretations in interspecies interactions: I used to regard the cat's hatred of traveling as a reflection of my own neurotic resistance to change, but cats are predators, territorial animals who become decreasingly confident the farther they get from their home territory, so repeatedly uprooting her from her familiar environs has probably not been a nuisance but something more like cruel.

And yet somehow this animal and I have learned, on some level, to understand one another. We coexist. Although I love to plunge my nose into her fur when she comes in from a chilly day and inhale deeply of the crisp wintry tang of the Coldcat Smell, the cat does not like this one bit, and flees me. For a while I would chase her around the house yelling "Gimme a little whiff!" and she would slink behind the couch to hide from my hateful touch. But eventually I realized that this was wrong of me. In the end a compromise was reached: now I let her in and pretend to have no interest whatsoever in smelling her, and go read on the couch, and after not more than a minute or so the cat will casually approach me and deign to be smelt. I really should be no less impressed by this accord than if I'd successfully communicated with a Paleolithic Papuan tribesman or decoded a message from the stars.

I've read that feng shui advises keeping a pet to maintain the chi of your house or apartment when you're not there; the very presence of an animal enlivens and charges the space. Although I suspect feng shui of being high-end hooey, I have learned, when my cat's been temporarily put up elsewhere, that a house without a cat in it feels very different from a house with one. It feels truly empty, inanimate, dead. It gives me some foreboding of how my life will feel after this cat is gone. We don't know what goes on inside an animal's head; we may doubt whether they have anything we'd call consciousness, and we can't know how much they understand or what their emotions feel like. I will never know what, if anything, that cat thinks of me. But I can tell you this much: a man who is in a room with a cat—whatever else we might say about that man—is not alone.

The Strange Situation

Abstract

My mother likes to tell a story about the time she volunteered me for a psychological study as an infant. "The psychologists at Johns Hopkins University laughed because [you] played with all their toys," she wrote in my baby book. "Two and three at a time, so they couldn't write down that [you] preferred any." Mom, being a mom, thought of this anecdote as evidence of my precocious curiosity and creativity. I, as an adult, sometimes thought of it as a sort of predictor of, or metaphor for, my romantic life: I wasn't about to commit to any one thing when there were so many tantalizing options available. I wanted to sample everything, have as much fun as possible, play with all the toys.

I had just broken up with the first girlfriend I'd been willing to call a "girlfriend" in years—or, rather, had left her no choice but to break up with me—and had finally decided that I might have what psychologists call attachment issues. I was reading a book about the history of attachment theory when I came across a description of a famous experiment conducted in the late '60s, Mary Ainsworth's "strange situation," that included the detail: "At one end of the room was a child's chair heaped with and surrounded by toys."[1] When I mentioned this to my mother, she said: "Ainsworth! That was the name of the researcher."

When therapists or social workers learn that I was one of the original subjects of the strange situation, they react in the way that a more general audience might if they were to learn I'd played one of the kids in *The Goonies*. The strange situation is still the most widely used lab setup in developmental psychology. The subject of the study was not, as it turns out, toy preference. What the researchers were observing were my reactions to my mother: what I did when she left the room, when she returned, when a stranger entered. (Mom tells me I didn't cry when she left and started to crawl toward her when she came back, but got distracted by a toy.) It's now the standard method of evaluating the attachment bond between infants and mothers, the way IQ tests are used to measure intelligence. It classifies infants into three distinct attachment patterns, which have proven to be disturbingly stable in longitudinal studies, meaning that most of us are still classified the same way we would've been in infancy—e.g., an infant who acts unconcerned when his mother leaves and ignores her when she returns might, as an adult, be reluctant to call the woman he's dating a "girlfriend," or subtly maneuver her into leaving him.

This probably ought not to come as shocking news to those of us reared in the post-Freudian world, which tells us we're all shaped and driven by the unremembered past, but it's still disquieting to see it borne out by hard data, or in your own life. I had told my friends that if this most recent relationship didn't work out, it might be time to accept that I didn't really want to be in a relationship at all. At age forty-seven, I'd never so much as lived with a woman, let alone been married. Summer was undeniably over; I now found myself living in an increasingly chilly vacation cabin with my partner in what had been by far the longest-term relationship of my life, a nineteen-year-old cat who was succumbing to senility and kidney failure. The cat had been given a year or two to live just about two years ago. She'd recently stopped using the sanctioned litter box and was now urinating on the carpet, the furniture, the woodstove, my record albums, even on the sofa right next to me when I was reading. My life now consisted of watching the cat like a raptor at all times, leaping up and whisking her outside whenever she started to pee, and then feeling ashamed for scaring her. The cat had taken to sitting up in the rafters, looking down at me as though I were a volatile lunatic. These are circumstances conducive to reflection.

We've all arrived at those moments when we look up from our lives and ask: *Why am I this person I would rather not be? Where exactly did things go wrong? How did I end up alone in this cabin with a demented and incontinent cat?* But, unlike most people, I was in a rare and oddly privileged position, having clinical data available about my infant self—what I imagined as my essential self, uncontaminated by experience, a control me. Somewhere in an old cardboard box or metal filing cabinet or on a piece of microfilm was a record of my attachment classification at eleven months, like a snapshot of the primordial universe. Mine is one of the first generations in history that could conceivably have had access to such information—or, probably, that would've cared. So that gray autumn, as I tended my senescent cat, I undertook a research project of my own: to track down the specific study in which I'd been a subject and find the raw data on myself from 1968.

To this end I enlisted the aid of my friend Margot, a professional science reporter. Margot's broken stories about strains of plague that could wipe us all out inside a month, but spends most of her time on what she calls cute-robot and "critter" stories. Not for nothing do they pay Margot, it turns out: within a couple hours of my asking her advice, she'd forwarded me more information than I would've unearthed in a year of poking around online myself. She sent me links and contact information for the archivists at the library of Johns Hopkins University, where the experiment was conducted, the Center for the History of Psychology at the University of Akron, where

Mary Ainsworth's papers are stored, and for one of Ainsworth's former grad students, Mary Main, who was still alive and professionally active. Margot, an implacable researcher, urged me not to give up until I knew the data was either inaccessible or destroyed.

"NPR aired a documentary by a guy who found the medical records of his own childhood lobotomy," she said, by way of encouragement. "He found a photo of himself with a knife in his eyeball, as I recall."

I also asked Margot's advice about my cat situation. She and her husband had owned a cat with a spraying problem so severe that they'd stopped inviting people over and consulted a pet psychologist. Margot suggested it might be a physical problem; she said she'd see a vet. She recommended I find one who would come to my house to euthanize the cat if necessary. When her own cat had been diagnosed with cancer, Margot was unable to bring herself to have it put to sleep, and it was now exiled to the backyard, where it pawed at the window, yowling stridently, so that Margot had to brace herself before walking into her own kitchen to make coffee every morning. She warned me that I would soon be grappling with cat-sized versions of some major moral and philosophical questions.

I don't know how much the past can tell you about yourself, or whether such understanding is of much use in trying to change. But it's become evident to me, in midlife, that my own history of intimate relationships—not wanting to choose, trying everything, never settling—may not have been the kind of experiment I thought it was, either. Its true subject may not have been all the alluring playthings I found so diverting but the thing that wasn't there, that I was pretending I didn't miss.

Introduction

That children are attached to their mothers may not sound like a discovery on par with the double helix. But only a couple of generations ago, the dogma among psychoanalysts was that infants' inner lives were ruled by internal fantasies—good versus evil breasts, Oedipal intrigues and parricides—not stuff that happened out in real life. And the conventional wisdom among behavioral psychologists, who must've made fun dads, was that children not only didn't need affection but could be actively damaged by it; mothers were cautioned against the hazards of kissing and cuddling, and warned not to feed their babies every time they cried or go to them when they woke in the night, lest they reinforce the behavior.

The father of attachment theory, John Bowlby, saw well-nourished children waste away when they were separated from their mothers for long periods during World War II. He posited that attachment was a primary drive, innate as aggression or libido: infants have an instinctive predisposition to attach to their mothers in order to protect themselves, in the same way that goslings "imprint" on the first thing they see (a phenomenon frequently observed in animated cartoons, as when baby chicks glom onto some inappropriate maternal figure like Foghorn Leghorn). You've probably seen photos of Harry Harlow's famous piteous-baby-monkey experiments: infant rhesus monkeys clinging to soft, carpeted dummy mothers, which they preferred to bare metal mothers that dispensed food, effectively refuting behaviorist claims that attachment was all about feeding, not feeling. But because human beings are animals with complex brains and long maturation periods, the development of attachment can be interrupted or distorted, affecting our future capacity for intimacy.

There was no way of objectively observing or measuring attachment until Bowlby's protégé, Mary Ainsworth, developed the strange situation in the late sixties at Johns Hopkins (the same university I would attend as an adult). Ainsworth later said that she and a colleague thought it up in about half an hour. It's an elegant twenty-minute lab procedure, staged in a room with two chairs, a door, and a one-way mirror. It consists of a sequence of eight orchestrated "episodes," including separations from and reunions with the mother, as well as the introduction of a stranger, both with and without the mother present. The toys my mom remembered were there to arouse the infant's curiosity and desire to explore; the mother's absence, and the appearance of the stranger, were meant to inhibit exploratory behavior and trigger his instinct to cling to the comfort of his mother.* Infants' reactions to all these stimuli were recorded in minute and quantifiable detail: observers watching through the one-way mirror took written notes and/or dictated them into a tape recorder, with a beep at fifteen-second intervals providing a timeline; the floor was divided into a grid for the precise measurement of the infant's every movement toward and away from his mother. All this data was then crunched and collated every which way imaginable using punch cards and room-sized computers.

In a graph of the subjects' scores, you can see infants clustering into three distinct groups, like stars falling into the main sequence, supergiants, and white dwarfs: (1) secure attachment and two types of insecure attachment, (2) avoidant and (3) anxious (also sometimes called "ambivalent").[2] In normal populations about 60 percent of infants are securely attached, with the remaining third falling into one of the two insecure categories.† Significantly, these results correlated well with months of observations Ainsworth had conducted in the subjects' homes.

---

* Ainsworth used the male pronoun to refer to infants in order to clearly distinguish them from their mothers, and I'm following the same convention for the same reason.

† Although avoidant and anxious attachment are less-than-ideal adaptations, they're still normal variations. (Only a rare fourth category later identified as "disorganized," characteristic of children from very dysfunctional family backgrounds, is considered pathological.) Also, bear in mind that these classifications aren't a rigid taxonomy but a spectrum: someone might be basically securely attached but have some avoidant or anxious tendencies.

In videos of the strange situation, you can see Bowlby's hypothesis that children use their mothers as a "secure base" for exploration enacted: securely attached children happily investigate the room and the toys, constantly looking back at their mothers for reassurance that it's safe to proceed. Although they cry when their mothers leave the room, they're easily comforted when they return. It's an infant's reaction on reunion with the mother that's the most telling of his classification. An avoidantly insecure child can look precociously independent, exploring fearlessly and displaying a curious lack of distress when his mother leaves, but when the mother returns, he may start to go toward her but then avert his eyes, act distracted, or draw away from her attempts to comfort him—he snubs her. An anxiously insecure child is too preoccupied with his mother to explore much at all, and gets extremely upset by her departure. Even when the mother comes back, he remains angry and inconsolable, twisting and kicking to get out of her arms, slapping away any toys proffered, as if her physical presence somehow can't compensate for her unforgivable absence.

It all sounds so arbitrary and inconsequential: one baby squirms, one cries, another shies away. But Margot forwarded me one longitudinal study showing that 72 percent of people in their twenties were still classified, as measured by the Adult Attachment Interview,* in the same way they had been at six months.[3] Those

* Obviously researchers can't run the strange situation on adults, few of whom still reliably cry when their mothers leave the room, so instead they ask them about their own childhoods and relationship histories using self-reporting techniques like the Adult Attachment Interview (AAI). This isn't a simple quiz like the ones in self-help books; subjects' attachment classifications are based less on the content than on a linguistic analysis of their answers. (Avoidantly insecure people have a hard time recalling clear details about their childhoods or composing an intelligible narrative about it, and tend to minimize the importance of

infinitesimal gestures resonate through the decades, echoing in our flirtations, fights, and breakups. Pretending not to notice the mother's return becomes not calling after an intimate weekend; inconsolable crying at being abandoned turns into sixteen texts in a row sent after midnight. Through the attachment process, infants form what psychologists call an "internal working model," an unconscious template for all their future relationships, which is why your girlfriend or husband sometimes seems to be reacting in a crazily inappropriate or disproportionate way, as if to someone other than you, and why you cannot seem to stop acting insane in relationships even when you know you are acting insane.

Adults who are classified as avoidant tend to separate sex and affection, fucking for fun instead of love, and are likelier to have multiple relationships or marriages. At an extreme, they may suffer from what the authors of one paper call "melancholic sexuality" or "the sexuality of despair," which they describe as "a cold arctic-like desert unwarmed by human relationship that barely achieves expression."*[4] The anxiously attached, by contrast, use sex to get the affection they're starved for, and long to merge totally with their partners; they're always scaring people off with the intensity of their need. (You might caricature these types as the guy who can't commit and the clingy girl—and these styles do seem to correlate, to some extent, with gender.) Interestingly, neither the avoidant

---

relationships; the anxiously insecure are still embroiled in the past, their accounts angry and incoherent.) The high correlation between strange situation and AAI classifications is obviously suggestive, although some killjoys like Margot want to know what makes us so sure these two different procedures are measuring the same thing.

* Holy cow! This passage is so florid and incoherent and bizarrely atypical of the clinical literature that it's hard to read as anything other than some researcher's thinly veiled seething over a cheating ex.

nor the anxious are compatible with their own types, whereas avoidant/anxious couples can be depressingly stable—those couples who endlessly break up and get together again, or live miserably ever after.[5] Some researchers have pointed out that people may play different roles in different relationships: sometimes you're the one who flees, sometimes you're the one who clings. Those who are insecurely attached in infancy are likely not only to have similar issues in their adult relationships but also to repeat the same pattern with their own children: one survey of studies involving hundreds of mother-infant pairs showed that 75 percent of mothers and infants matched up in their secure-versus-insecure classifications.[6] Since the strange situation was first developed, researchers have tried to correlate attachment classification with everything else they could think of—relationships and marriage, school and work performance, addiction, grief, political ideology and religiosity*—and suffice it to say the securely attached are generally healthier, happier, and more functional in just about every area of life.

Which must be nice for them. My own life increasingly revolves around accommodating the declining health of a small animal. Per Margot's suggestion, I took my cat to the vet, who diagnosed her as nineteen years old. He advised against euthanizing her so long as she was still eating and mobile. (I didn't tell the vet that it would not occur to me to have the cat euthanized so long as she was still right-side out.) For the time being, she seems content to sit purring on my lap seventeen hours a day, occasionally pissing on my things. Margot recommended I buy "puppy pads" for the cat, so there are now little throw rugs of absorbent diaperlike material placed around my house, which some might view as a deterioration of

---

* Someone's even run the strange situation on dogs and cats, with unsurprising results: dogs actually do appear to be attached to human beings; cats are in it for the cat food.

basic living standards. I've made the executive decision to abandon the cat's special medicated kidney-health cat food and go back to Fancy Feast. Albacore tuna, bacon, fuck it—whatever the cat wants. I had assumed at first that she was entering a swift terminal decline, but instead she seems to have leveled off at a new, fairly low plateau. It's possible this is just what my life is like now.

I am managing the stress of the present situation with some medications that were prescribed, though not specifically for me, and by meticulously building a plastic model of a well-known fictional spacecraft, a behavior so obviously regressive there is no need to comment on it. I still catch myself saving up factoids and anecdotes to tell my ex-girlfriend—that this month's full moon is called the Beaver Moon, that I got published in Dutch, that I ran into "Pappy" again—but in the short time since our breakup I've also been carrying on a torrid and voluble strangers-on-a-train correspondence with a doctoral candidate in philosophy, asked out a woman in a bar in Delaware whose last name I don't know, gone on a date with a jaw-droppingly busty grad student in social work, spent a weekend in a hotel room doing the *Times* crossword naked with an Albertan chess player, and, throughout, have been lusting pathetically after a checkout girl at my local supermarket whose hair is a lustrous tangled Pre-Raphaelite mass of Celtic red and whose rump is full and jutting in her taut khaki Food King–issue pants. What is wrong with me? Am I an insane person? Is this—*the sexuality of despair*?

One morning at my local library I realized that the sleeve of my jacket smelled like cat piss. "You should fix that as soon as possible," my friend Kevin wrote me very seriously. "That is the kind of thing that can start to define you if it goes on for too long."

Methods

A couple of my female friends once proposed that everyone should be required to wear a T-shirt printed with a slogan disclosing their problem (e.g., I AM AN EMOTIONAL ROBOT) so that you would be forewarned before disrobing with them. When I first read about attachment theory, I thought that here, for those who wanted it, was such a T-shirt. Think of the billions of dollars and countless hours that people have squandered on horoscopes and tarot cards, self-help books about Games and Rules, Martians versus Venusians, all in an effort to figure out what type of person they are, which type their partners are, whom they're compatible with and whom to avoid. They would all have been better advised to read any pop-psychology book on attachment.

There are plenty of such books now, complete with charts of the cognitive and behavioral habits characteristic of each attachment style and questionnaires to determine your own. I've watched my friends pass these around in bars like Internet quizzes to determine which character from *Barney Miller* you are. Some of them refuse to look at them, like cartoon Bushmen spooked by photos of themselves. It's fun to armchair-classify your friends and exes. But the real question—especially if you happen to have been a subject of the experiment that established these classifications—is: *Which one am I?*

Without access to the data, I can't know how I was classified. But, based on my mother's description of my behavior in the study, and my entire relationship history, I have my suspicions.

"You were a very alert eight- and eleven-month-old* and loved playing with the toys they gave you," Mom wrote me.

> At one point in testing I picked you up and walked around the room. You looked at all the toys that were there and then settled down to study the ball with the butterfly inside it. The researcher commented on how much you loved that toy and said I

* The strange situation was conducted in two separate phases: a home observation and the lab procedure.

> should get you one, but I never saw another toy like that. When I left the room while the strange person (Ainsworth herself) was there, you were playing with the ball and didn't fuss. You entered into a baby talk conversation with her. When I returned to the room you started toward me, then looked at the ball and went back to it and continued playing with it. When it was time to go I picked you up and we left without a fuss on your part.

It would be a low thing to use one's own mother's testimony against her, but I have to say that when Mom wrote this account for me, the line *you started toward me, then looked at the ball and went back to it* sounded like the classic behavior of an avoidantly insecure infant. But I am not remotely qualified to interpret this account, which isn't even data but a personal recollection written decades after the fact. And that interpretation also jibes a little too neatly with my latest narrative about myself, confirming my fear that I'm somehow impaired in forming attachments. As with horoscopes or descriptions of rare medical disorders, it's easy to project yourself into any of the attachment classifications. If I really wanted to know the answer, I'd need the original data.

Margot and I learned right away that gaining access to that data was going to be a lot trickier than I'd anticipated. Mary Ainsworth had been something of a hardass about confidentiality, it turned out: she didn't want to repay people who'd volunteered their children as subjects, allowed her into their homes, and offered up intimate details of their lives by labeling some of them as "insensitive" mothers or their children as "insecurely attached." All subjects in the strange situation were informed that the data was "subject to anonymity of participants," meaning that my mom would've signed a consent form waiving any future access to it. All names, addresses, and parents' occupations were deleted in order to anonymize the data. "It's actually pretty impressive, how many safeguards she took to ensure that her promise to the parents, that it would all be anonymous, would be kept," wrote Margot, who is unrelenting at ferreting out information someone else has taken pains to conceal. "You have your work cut out for you." All of which meant I would have to resort to subterfuge.

"I figured that would be your response," sighed Margot. She declined to enter, even in a spirit of harmless fun, into any hypothetical discussion of duplicity, ruses, Viennese pseudonyms, glue-on Vandykes, or any other such schemes to obtain the information illicitly. "It's such anathema to my profession I don't want to discuss it, no matter how jokingly," she said. Basically, Margot is Commissioner Gordon and I am Batman: ultimately on the same team, but pursuing our ends through very different means.

I was stymied until the day after Thanksgiving, when my mother stopped by my cabin while I happened to have Mary Ainsworth's 1978 book, *Patterns of Attachment*, open in front of me. For the first time in my hearing, Mom recalled that the study we'd participated in had had something to do with object permanence, the phenomenon on which the game peekaboo is predicated: the recognition that things, and people, still exist when you can't see them. As it happened, I had just been reading about the very first follow-up studies to Ainsworth's original experiment, and there it was, right in front of me: sample 2 of the strange situation, "The development of the concept of the object as related to infant-mother attachment," published in 1970. It had been conducted not by Mary Ainsworth (though, as Mom recalled, she had assisted, playing the role of the stranger) but by one of her graduate students, Silvia Bell. It was a strange feeling to come across a list of all the toys used in the initial studies and to see there, under samples 1 and 2, "plastic butterfly ball."[7] There it was—the toy that Mom says so entranced me at eleven months, like an object from a dream. Stranger still to read, in the "methods" section of Bell's paper:

> The sample consisted of 33 subjects, 21 males and 12 females, of middle-class parents. . . . All were full-term babies, in good

health, who had normal births. Two of the boys had been adopted by their present mothers when they were between 2 and 3 months of age.[8]

That was me. I was one of those two adopted boys.

Have I mentioned that I was adopted? I was: I was put up for adoption by my biological mother when I was a day or two old, and in foster care until my parents adopted me a couple of months later. Although Bell's paper mentions adoption up front, she doesn't consider it as a factor in attachment. The effect of adoption isn't addressed in Ainsworth's book, either, although she examines a lot of other potential factors in attachment: class, birth weight, Apgar scores, and whether or not the mothers worked. Maybe this was a function of the conventional wisdom of the time; my own parents didn't make any big deal of my having been adopted, though they were always honest and matter-of-fact about it. For a long time I thought the only lingering symptom of having been given up at birth was the wrenching pity I felt for discarded objects and uneaten food, a pity that extends even to products I fear are likely to be unpopular or rejected. (Whenever I see a generic soft drink called Dr. Perky on the shelves of the Food King, I feel so sorry for it I can barely stand to live.) It wasn't until I found myself still single in my forties, long after all my friends—even the most obvious misfits, womanizers, sots and misogynists—had successfully mated and reproduced, that I started to wonder whether it hadn't had some more significant, lasting effect.

Since I was a kid, the self-help/therapeutic/pharmaceutical industries have successfully pathologized every facet of the human condition, from being bored in school to hating winter. Adoptees are now described as suffering a sort of post-traumatic disorder. One of the books I read on the subject was called *The Primal Wound* and had a cover illustration of a swaddled infant enclosed in what looked like either the titular injury or a vulva pulled open with retractors. It wasn't something you wanted to be seen reading on the subway. Another cover showed a toddler behind barbed wire. A lot of these books are written in a sort of hushed prose ("You might be feeling unsafe right now"), as if intended to soothe a hysteric. But their descriptions of the relationship troubles typical of adoptees were not unfamiliar: multiple relationships or marriages, brief but intense affairs, devastating breakups, attractions to emotionally unavailable partners, and the sabotage of stable relationships.

Still, let's not make too much of this factor: it would never occur to me to call my parents my "adoptive" parents. My own childhood was spent not behind barbed wire but on the sofa eating Pop-Tarts and watching *Ultraman*. About the worst thing that ever happened to me was Math. Although it would be a relief to be able to attribute my relationship problems to something that happened back when I was still blameless, the clinical literature doesn't back me up; there doesn't seem to be much correlation between adoption and insecure attachment unless there's a previous history of neglect or abuse.*[9] I have several friends who were also adopted and are now, to all appearances, happily married.

"Hey, I know you've focused on adoption," wrote Margot, "but did you note, in that twenty-year long-term study, that one of the things that can make people switch to becoming insecurely attached is the death of a parent?" My father died of cancer when I was just a couple of years out of college, as Margot well knows. At the time I didn't think I took this too hard; I was just angry and depressed and drank too much for a couple decades. "I imagine that watching a loved one die is the kind of experience that could give anyone pause about getting too close to someone else," Margot wrote, "even if it's someone they really want to be close to."

I wondered whether this line might not be an allusion to our

---

* There is a slightly higher incidence of insecure attachment in transnational adoptions.

own history: my father had died only a few weeks before Margot and I started dating. I should also have mentioned that Margot and I were once romantically involved. We went out for four years: we broke up once, forgot why we'd broken up, got back together and then remembered. I'd known her since she was twelve years old (though I stress for the record that our involvement did not begin at this time). We used to have a routine, back then, where I would try to keep a straight face while she said, looking steadily at me with her intelligent, grave little face: "Timothy, I'm afraid you're just not living up to your full potential." She would say the same words to me over a decade later, through tears, the day we broke up.

I remember the first time I saw her as a young woman in college: I spotted her from the back seat of a car as she was crossing Baltimore's Charles Street, her auburn hair shining copper in the sun against an azure sweater.* It was one of those moments old married couples enshrine in story, where the world goes still: *I knew right then that she was the one.* Whenever I hear people say things like *Marrying that woman was the best decision I ever made* or *I don't know where I'd be without her,* I think: *You'd be me. I'm the guy who didn't make the best decision he ever made.* Once, when a coworker of Margot's said that if she were to learn her husband were a pedophile, it would be a "deal breaker" for her marriage, Margot said: "That's funny—I don't remember the words 'deal breaker' being in my wedding vows." Hearing this, it occurred to me that a man would be very lucky to go through life with a woman like Margot at, and on, his side. But it turns out you can learn to live without anyone.

Instead I ended up with this cat, whom I often call, in deference to her age and dowager status, Mrs. The Cat. I've now jerry-rigged various ramps and structures around the house to enable her, in her

* Margot disputes this memory; she says the first time we saw each other was in the lobby of an apartment building.

enfeebled condition, to get up on top of the sorts of things cats like to be on top of: the floor speakers, the pump organ, the woodstove. I've duct-taped a box to the top of the speaker, with raised sides like a hospital bed, so that she will not slide off of it in her sleep and plop onto the floor, which startles her and makes me sad. As a backup, I've padded the floor around the speaker with cushions. But these adaptations work for only a few days before her condition declines further and she no longer needs them. Mostly she now lies on the carpet by the sliding glass door in a neat loaf, asleep in a trapezoid of sun. Occasionally I check to make sure she's still breathing. Late at night she prowls around the house yowling—a mournful yowl, a yowl of the soul. We are about to enter a new phase involving biweekly injections of subcutaneous fluid, which I do not expect to improve man-cat relations one bit.

In an email titled "So I Can't Stop Researching," Margot told me that my study might've been part of Silvia Bell's dissertation, which could be downloaded or ordered on microfilm for $38. She also informed me that that Silvia Bell was not only alive but still practicing, easily contactable through the Baltimore Washington Center for Psychotherapy and Psychoanalysis. Although I'd embarked on this project determined to find the data on my infant self, now that I'd come unexpectedly close to the source, I found myself balking. Maybe some things ought to remain unquantified. I could easily have arranged to take the Adult Attachment Interview myself, but after a few cursory inquiries I'd dropped it. I've never wanted to know my IQ score or Myers-Briggs type, either. If I ever have a terminal illness, the way I'd prefer to learn about it is by dying. What if I were to find out I'd been classified as avoidant: How would that help? Do I really want to see a picture of myself with a knife in my eye?

"It seems to me that your mom is the one who should be apprehensive," wrote Margot. "Because isn't any attachment problem supposedly firmly rooted, at least in part, in how the mother acts, or fails to act?" It's true that the strange situation is an evaluation not just of the child but of the mother as well; the literature often refers to them jointly as a "dyad." Margot, a mother of two, masochistically imagined some observer's pitiless clinical transcription of her own parenting:

1:03 P.M.: Baby tries to crawl, falls on face, begins to cry. Mother finishes pouring coffee, adds sugar, stirs, before speaking to baby.
1:08 P.M.: Mother briefly plays peekaboo with baby, who loses interest and examines a shoe.
1:11 P.M.: Baby holds out toy monkey and tries to engage mother. Mother is looking at Weather Channel to check the snow and the commute.

"I can imagine all this vividly," she shuddered.

The security of an infant's attachment to his mother doesn't correlate with the traits you might assume it would; it has less to do with what we think of as "warmth" than with a subtler quality that Ainsworth called "sensitivity"—the mother's ability to read her child's signals, intuit his wants, and respond to them quickly and appropriately.[10] (You can imagine a mother who's demonstratively affectionate, cuddling and nuzzling and going *O whooza little boozhy boozhy boo* when what her kid obviously wants is to be let alone to play—the mother acting on her own needs instead of her child's.) "There is a great difference between maternal warmth and maternal sensitivity," Ainsworth said, "and it took me a long time to appreciate it."[11]

Essentially, what she called "sensitivity" involves empathy: paying attention to the baby's cues, letting him take the initiative, recognizing him as an autonomous individual. It may go without saying that people who are more reflective and self-aware themselves tend to be better at this. Researchers have traced the mechanism of cause and effect here to show how reciprocating an infant's signals, or failing to, can reinforce or inhibit their responses. A rather mean-sounding study that involved getting mothers not to smile back at their babies when they smiled found that the infants not only stopped smiling but began "fussing" and actively avoiding eye contact with their mean unsmiling mothers—elegantly demonstrating how the desire for connection can be turned into its (apparent) opposite by a lack of reinforcement.[12]

Yes, this is all unavoidably touchy stuff, smacking of yet more mom blaming when moms have already been blamed for everything from overachievement to schizophrenia and are happy just to get a freaking phone call on Mother's Day. My own mom's official policy re my research is that she supports me in answering whatever questions I may have and will be interested to hear about anything I learn. But since Mom's official policy toward all things is 100% positivity and support, you never know with Mom. But I still feel a little guilty; wouldn't it subtly poison your relationship with your mother to learn that her parenting had been second-guessed or found deficient by experts?

"On the other hand," said Margot, "what if your mom's description suggests you were not firmly attached, but you looked at the original data and they thought you were?" This question gave me pause. I was prepared to learn potentially unpleasant truths about myself, but less prepared for pleasant ones. When I'd described my mom's recollection of my behavior in the strange situation to a dinner table full of psychoanalysts, they told me it sounded like pretty healthy exploratory behavior. Embarrassingly, I was disappointed. Although it would be troubling to learn I'd been classed as avoidant, it would also be a kind of relief, somehow validating. "Whereas if I was securely attached as an infant," I told Margot, "it would mean that I'm not a victim of some primal loss or trauma but just another dickhead."

"My point exactly," she said. "Even if you were traumatized, and even if you had some scientifically documented evidence for this, you are still ultimately responsible for any dickhead behavior. Inasmuch as anyone can be held responsible for anything," she added—"Does free will exist, blah blah blah."

Well. There's a case to be made that we're all so many wind-up toys set in motion by our pasts, colliding and battering each other to pieces. Some days self-awareness mostly seems like a source of embarrassment, enabling you to watch yourself fucking up with greater clarity. I found my own tendencies in relationships enumerated with humiliating accuracy in self-help books' chapters on the avoidant type: maintaining emotional distance, not admitting that a relationship is a "real" relationship, withdrawing after intimate times together, feeling controlled, amplifying your partner's faults, imagining there's some other perfect person out there, pining over idealized exes. It's even characteristic of avoidants, once they've successfully driven off their partners, to belatedly experience all the feelings of deep attachment they'd been repressing. Reading these books was so upsetting that I kept setting them aside to read John Keegan's horrific descriptions of wounds inflicted at Waterloo and the Somme instead.[13]

Margot wasn't buying this deterministic bullshit. "I don't know," she said. "The 'science' of all this seems pretty squishy." Margot's a skeptic on the social sciences and disdains the sort of reporters who announce the existence of a "romance gene" based on genetic variants found in monogamous prairie voles. Human personalities are complex and messy; it's impossible to isolate a single variable or trace causality in an individual history. As Margot asked, "What do the observations of some stranger, a self-proclaimed expert, from forty years ago on your infant behavior in a completely artificial situation mean for you?"*

---

* Margot is not the first to charge the strange situation's methodology with squishiness. There was a lot of initial skepticism about the study, much of it doubting that such a contrived artificial situation could fairly represent the normal interaction of a mother and child. The particular study in which I was a subject was taken to task because the same person (Silvia Bell) had determined both the object-permanence scores and strange situation classifications. Ainsworth herself always emphasized that the data collected in the controlled setting of the strange situation could only be understood in the context of much longer observations of infants and mothers interacting in their own homes.

I'd taken the 72 percent stability of attachment classifications in that longitudinal study as depressing evidence of the determinism of early experience. But Margot, an optimist by policy if not temperament, chooses to look at the glass as 28 percent full. Like most things in life, attachment is more easily changed for the worse, mostly by major stressors like divorce, abuse, the serious illness (including mental illness) or death of a parent. But kids really are resilient, and can become securely attached to a foster parent, an aunt or a grandparent, even a teacher or a coach. And parents have been known, in some instances, to get their shit together: that same longitudinal study cites the case of a child who developed a chronic illness and whose parents responded "with consistent sensitive care," after which her classification changed from insecure to secure. "So it's not as if something that was one way in childhood dooms you forever to one state of being," Margot concluded. "At least, if you believe all this 'science.'"

Eventually you get sick of thinking about yourself. The last thing you want is to end up carrying armloads of self-help books home from the library, blathering on about your Journey, still bitterly blaming the tiny senile people who were once your parents for your middle-aged life. In the end I gambled on honesty: I wrote to Dr. Bell care of the Baltimore Washington Center for Psychotherapy and Psychoanalysis and told her I was a writer working on an essay about attachment and also, it happened, a former subject of her dissertation study. I said I'd be interested in talking to her about attachment in general and her own research in particular. I enclosed a copy of my first book and mailed it off. I did not mention in my letter that I'd learned that we had the same birthday.

"Do you really believe you have 'attachment issues'?" Margot finally asked me. I would've thought that Margot, of all people, would know. Back when she and I were dating, I figured I'd probably get married someday for the same reason I assume I'll probably die:

everybody else eventually seems to. At that time I treated relationship talks like getting sent to the principal's office: you just say whatever it seems like they want to hear so you can get out of there as quickly as possible. But as Margot pressed the question of our long-term plans, I started having bad dreams. The word *doomed* started coming up a lot in our conversations. Finally I got infatuated with someone who was safely unavailable long enough for Margot to find out.

My last girlfriend had been surprisingly patient with my panic at finding myself in a relationship. She'd likened me to a fainting goat, those animals with a genetic defect that causes them to topple comically over when startled. It's hard not to laugh in a shamefaced way when you see videos of it: it's such a pitiful, ridiculous thing to do. How could such a maladaptive mechanism ever have evolved?

Mary Ainsworth took pains to dispel any notion that she'd identified any preexisting "types" of children; *all* infants are naturally attached to their mothers. Even the ones who remain outwardly indifferent when their mothers leave the room show the elevated heart rates associated with distress.[14] All children have the same need for attention, but because that need is sometimes ignored, rebuked, or inconsistently met, some of them learn coping strategies to maximize contact with the mother while minimizing the possibility of rejection—by suppressing their need, redirecting it, or reacting against it. We adopt these behaviors because they work, more or less, when we're seven months old. But it can take up to forty-seven years to notice that they aren't working so well anymore. We erect increasingly elaborate structures to prop up and protect something that's essentially failing, like this system of cat ramps, boxes, and cushions that's turned my home into a Caligarian cat hospice.

I understand that there's something I'm missing out on. The secure infant-mother relationship is said to provide a "secure base for exploration," and according to attachment researcher Mary Main we are happiest living our lives this way—saying *I love you* and kissing each other good-bye in the morning, venturing out into the uncaring world to have all kinds of adventures, then returning home to share our daily pocketful of collected anecdotes and complaints.[15] An unshared life feels scarily as if it might not be occurring. Driving through a corridor of autumnal color or a cawing gauntlet of crows, I have an impulse to tell someone about it. Who am I going to call when this cat dies?

There was a night not long after we broke up when Margot called my cabin because there was some footage on TV of Nixon playing the piano that she knew I'd want to see. "I let the phone ring and ring but no one picked up," she wrote me later in a postcard. I'd been out having dinner with a neighbor when she called. "Inside, my heart keeps ringing and ringing," she wrote. "I can't hang up but there's nobody home." That was seventeen years ago, but I still think about that night sometimes.

One of the last times I saw Margot, she had embarked on a radical decluttering campaign, ruthlessly throwing out attic ephemera—the seating chart for her wedding, leaves pressed by long-dead aunts—and she asked me bluntly whether I'd like a box of my old love letters to her back. She figured that, as a writer, I might be able to use them. "Look," she said, seeing the expression on my face, "we have a relationship now, in the present. Isn't that more important than some love affair we had when I was nineteen?" What I really wanted was for Margot to clasp these letters to her breast on her deathbed, weeping with love and regret. But Margot is not one for maundering over the past. She always signs her emails:

Onward,
M.

Margot's right: the past doesn't exist. It's only a story, one we keep rewriting. If you'd asked me why she and I broke up right after it happened, I would've told you that although she said she wanted to marry me, she didn't seem to like anything about me. Ten years later I would've told you I was depressed and drinking too much and blew a good thing. These days I like to think it was because I'm avoidantly insecure. (Margot would tell you her own, much different story.) Maybe we just go through life telling ourselves one story after another to get through the days, replacing the old ones with newer ones as needed, like shoes. In the '50s, psychoanalysis promised to make sense of us with its unconscious complexes, dreams and free association; in the '60s, behaviorism explained it all through positive and negative reinforcement, food pellets and shocks; now attachment is in intellectual fashion, and seems like a fuller, more empirical explanation. No doubt a hundred years from now all these hypotheses will seem like crude approximations.

It'd be nice to believe we're replacing old stories with truer, more useful ones, spiraling asymptotically in on the Truth even if we'll never quite touch it. But I sometimes feel as if the older I get, the *less* sense life makes, and the more all attempts at explanation seem like fictions—that, in all honesty, I have no idea why anything happened or what it all meant. Some mornings I sit at my laptop over my first cup of coffee, trying to think of one true sentence I can write, staring into space with longer and longer pauses between typing, wondering what to make of this life. Why am I spending this cold autumn alone, waiting for a cat to die? Was it being given up for adoption? My father's death? Does free will exist blah blah blah? *It rings and rings but nobody's home.*

Results

Dear Mr. Kreider,

I was delighted to hear of your interest in attachment and in making contact with me after so many years. I did receive your book, as well as your letter, and would be quite pleased to speak with you. You may reach me directly either via email or, preferably, by calling my office.

Best,

Silvia Bell

"The last time she saw you, you were a wee babe," Margot exulted. "Now, a man, you return to face the one who sat in judgment of you. You are like the replicant in *Blade Runner* finding and confronting its maker." I hoped my interview with Dr. Bell would end more amicably than that one, but I had to admit our meeting felt portentous. On the phone, Dr. Bell told me I was the first of her former subjects ever to contact her. It occurred to me that to her I might represent a very narrow longitudinal study. We arranged to meet at her home office in Baltimore on the morning of Friday the fourteenth, which neither of us mentioned was Valentine's Day.

Silvia Bell introduced herself in the waiting room of her office, where I'd been studying a find-the-hidden-picture drawing in *Highlights* magazine that was either badly drawn or sadistically difficult. (I couldn't believe they were inflicting this puzzle on young children. Where was the fucking snake?) She was much younger than I'd expected—she told me later that she'd been *nineteen* when she started her doctoral program at Johns Hopkins. My mother remembered her as "a tiny thing," and she was still small and fine-boned, with a very un-old-ladylike mane of tawny hair going gray. I'd brought her some potted daffodils to thank her for seeing me.

"It's nice to meet you," I told her. "Though I guess we've met before."

"In a way," she said.

"I suppose I look different now," I said.

Dr. Bell's office is equipped with both chairs and the traditional couch. I opted for the chair. Maybe it was the setting, but it felt like an oddly ambiguous conversation; it was unclear to me, at least, whether I was approaching her as an interviewer or a patient.

Margot had advised me that scientists like to talk about science, so you should let them, because it gets them comfortable before you ask them your real questions. Dr. Bell's papers are couched in clinical language, but in person she's less circumspect about her real agenda, which was in formulating a theory of communication, and of mind. "My interest," she said, "has always been in *meaning*." (Whenever Dr. Bell says *meaning*, you can tell it's in italics.) "God forbid you would label it 'the growth of love,'" she said (words like *love* are considered unprofessionally mushy) but what she was really studying was the point at which a child begins to connect certain experiences and feelings—*meaning*—with another human being. Attachment isn't just about your relationships with others, she explained, but about your sense of self and of the world. "In the process of becoming attached to the mother," she explained, "the infant discovers not only that the mother has a mind but that *he* has a mind." I wondered whether attachment could shape your whole worldview; what seemed like an objective perception of the universe as indifferent or capricious might be something a lot more personal.

Without clever segue, I just came out and asked Dr. Bell whether I could find out how I'd been classified. She told me that she wouldn't be able to find that data even if she wanted to. "The first thing that you do the moment you refer somebody [for a study] is to create a number for them," she explained, "and you do not mix numbers with names or any identifying information." It would be hard to say whether I was disappointed; in a way it felt like calling someone you don't want to talk to and getting their voice mail.

"The only thing I will say," she confided, "is I *do* remember a Timothy in my study." ("The most beautiful words any reporter can hear," Margot had told me, "are 'I probably shouldn't be telling you this . . .'") "And I remember just a delightful experience." She laughed and looked, for a moment, like the nineteen-year-old girl she'd been when we first met, around this same time of year in 1968. "I don't have any details," she said, "but I do remember having a wonderful time with you. Just having fun. There was a lot of back-and-forth that was"—she smiled again, and I could see her remembering me—"you know, fun."

Dr. Bell's particular experiment had found a correlation between secure attachment and early development of object and person permanence. "The essence of my study relied on particular game I would have played with you," she explained, "which was a hide-and-seek game. And, um," she added, not unplayfully, "I thought that hiding and seeking seems to have some meaning for you in your life." I asked her if she could elaborate, but Dr. Bell was cagey. "I think in everybody's life hide-and-seek is a big deal," she said.

In general, psychologists aren't as fatalistic about the effect of early experience as they used to be back when "fixed by six" was the grim formula in child development. In her experience, Dr. Bell said, "the resilience of human beings is not something we can theoretically cap in any way." A catchword in psychology now is *epigenetic*, a term cribbed from biology, "meaning that you have phases," she explained, "and that what happens in one phase does impact the next, but the next is also an opportunity to rework the earlier phase. The question is: What happens next?"

Like most psychoanalysts, Dr. Bell is not in the business of handing out answers. "I think people turn to inquire about the past when they're stuck in the present in some way," she told me. It felt like a hint, as if she were trying to tell me the data I wanted was right in front of my face. Forty-six years later, we were still playing hide-and-seek. "It is a joy to be hidden," pediatrician and psychoanalyst D. W. Winnicott wrote, "but disaster not to be found."[16] The snake was hidden in the bark of the tree, it turned out. The giveaway was the dot of the eye.

I walked out of my interview feeling as if I'd gotten to have my one quick handshake talk with God, and He'd said, *Oh, yeah—I remember you. I always liked you, kid*, and given me a little sock on the arm. That Valentine's Day was one of those days of freakish, unexpected clemency you sometimes get in the dead of winter: the sun was shining and the latest heavy snow was thawing in a sloppy, exhilarating rush; hills of craggy black ice were still heaped up in supermarket parking lots, but you also had to leap over deep puddles and rivulets of meltwater everywhere. The world was a mess, the way your house gets messier when you're in the middle of a serious cleaning. It wasn't here yet, and wouldn't be for a couple more dark months to come, but that day it at least felt possible to believe in spring.

Discussion

Margot and I had been corresponding throughout most of our research project, but one night when I visited her city we sat up late talking long after her husband and kids had gone to bed. We were at her kitchen table, watching a late-April snow squall whirl down outside the window, a last fuck-you from a long, relentless winter. She still looked much the same to me as she did at eighteen—the same wry intelligence behind new, azure-armed glasses. Unbeknownst to me, Margot had been having a much worse time of it than I had that winter—"unbeknownst" because, unlike me, Margot isn't a complainer. Another difference between Margot and me is that when she finds herself doing things that she doesn't approve of, or that alarm her, she does something about it. When she started having anxiety attacks at age thirteen, she informed her parents she needed help and called a psychologist herself to make an appointment. When she quit drinking, she didn't join a twelve-step program; she just stopped. She'd always prided herself on being one of the few people she knew who wasn't in therapy or on medication. But recently, more for her family's sake than her own, she had warily sought professional help.

The first thing Margot did after she started on antidepressants was put her cat to sleep. "Any sane person would've had the cat killed long ago," she said. She could now walk into her own kitchen to make coffee in the morning without steeling herself first. My own cat had died over the winter—she slunk out of the house with sudden wily alacrity one afternoon, and later that day I found her down on the beach, awaiting her death with bushido stoicism. I probably should've left her there, but I couldn't let her drown or freeze to death or get eaten by coyotes, so I gathered her up and carried her back to the house. She felt bony and fragile, surprisingly light in my arms. She died late that night, and I buried her in the yard at dawn. In the days after the cat's death I received an unexpected number of condolences from friends, ex-girlfriends, ex-girlfriends' parents—even from women I hadn't known were still speaking to me, who'd always been on terms of formal enmity with the cat, like the wreaths dropped by Allied pilots at the Red Baron's funeral.

Margot had only been in treatment for a couple of weeks now, but already she'd noticed that people at work were treating her differently—having more intimate conversations with her, confiding in her, sending her links to poems. It made her wonder what she must've seemed like before. I could imagine that, if you didn't know Margot, she might seem a little severe—intimidating, even. She didn't seem like a different person to me now; she seemed very much Margot, but at one less remove—warmer, more unguarded, unabashedly happy to see me. Her demeanor was one of barely suppressed mirth, as though she were remembering a joke she knew I wouldn't get.

One reason people cling so loyally to their maladaptive patterns is that, once you've recognized them, the narrative you've constructed to rationalize them unravels and suddenly your whole life can look like a sad stupid waste. Lately I wanted to write formal letters of apology to everyone I'd ever dated. I wished I could tell them all, without its sounding like complete bullshit, that all my hurtful feints and dodges had been symptoms of love, however well disguised, as telltale as dilated eyes or bad poetry. Mostly I wanted to travel back in time and punch myself in the face forever. But we only travel through time one way, and all you can do, as Margot pointed out, is try to ensure that five years from now you won't want to come back and punch yourself in the present.

"If you really feel some need to atone to me," she told me, "instead of apologizing, you can get involved in a lasting intimate relationship. That's how you can make it up to me." I'd been afraid she would say something like this. *You're just not living up to your full potential.* It would be easier to travel back in time. The problem isn't that change is impossible; it's that it's really hard. We do have free will blah blah blah; we just hardly ever use it.

Margot waved aside my worries that I might be somehow essentially damaged or lacking. "You do have intimate relationships," she pointed out. "In fact, I would say you have more, and more intimate, relationships than anyone else I know." I guess what I am, like Margot and you and everyone else, is complicated. We all get lopped up, scarred or obstructed, and grow into complexly knotted shapes—stunted or twisted, lopsided or split, sometimes improbably beautiful, like trees growing on around barbed wire. A friend of mine used to say, "Perfect people are boring." And anyway, which would you rather be: securely attached, or *delightful*?

Margot assured me that she and I weren't as different as I thought. "It's not as if being with someone makes you any less alone," she said. I gave her an easy-for-you-to-say look. "I mean, sure it's nice to have someone care when you come home and complain about your day," she said. "But in the big ways, like in facing death, we're all on our own." She'd lately been having vertiginous spells of awareness of her own mortality: while loading the dishwasher she'd suddenly know, as surely as she could tell she was standing upright with her eyes closed, that she was going to die. Her decluttering campaign, she explained, was a way of facing this head-on. "People think that by clinging to all this stuff they can hold on to the past, stop time, and ward off death," she said. "I would like to do my part to smash that illusion. The past is gone. We're here now."

Margot thinks all my old letters to her are in a box upstairs at her parents' house in Alabama; she intends to get them for me the next time she's down there. That postcard she wrote the night she tried to call me, which used to convulse me with remorse, is in a slot in my desk in New York, an inert piece of cardboard. And the data on my infant self, my every telltale gesture transcribed one January day in 1968, is in some basement archive in Baltimore, or Akron, or Cambridge—or who knows, maybe it was sitting out in plain view on Silvia Bell's desk like the Purloined Letter the whole time. The past is gone. But we're here now, Margot and me, sitting together at this kitchen table tonight, talking hard about our problems, relationships, and therapy, while it keeps coming down outside. "The question is," as Dr. Bell said, "what happens next?"

Onward,

Citations

1. Mary D. Salter Ainsworth and Silvia M. Bell, "Attachment, Exploration, and Separation: Illustrated by the Behavior of One-Year-Olds in a Strange Situation." *Child Development* 41, no. 1 (March 1970): 53.
2. Mary D. Salter Ainsworth, Mary C. Blehar, Everett Walters, and Sally Wall, *Patterns of Attachment: A Psychological Study of the Strange Situation* (New York and London: Psychology Press and Taylor & Francis Group, 1978), 102: Fig. 10, "Contour Plot of Discriminant Scores."
3. Everett Waters, Susan Merrick, Dominique Treboux, Judith Crowell, and Leah Albersheim, "Attachment Security in Infancy and Early Adulthood: A 20-Year Longitudinal Study." *Child Development* 71, no. 3 (May/June 2000): 684–89.
4. B. Laschinger, C. Purnell, J. Schwartz, K. White, and R. Wingfield, "Sexuality and Attachment from a Clinical Point of View." *Attachment and Human Development* 6, no. 2 (June 2004): 156.
5. Lee A. Kirkpatrick and Keith E. Davis, "Attachment Style, Gender, and Relationship Stability: A Longitudinal Analysis." *Journal of Personality and Social Psychology* 66, no. 3 (March 1994): 502–12.
6. H. van IJzendoorn Marinus, "Adult Attachment Representations, Parental Responsiveness, and Infant Attachment: A Meta Analysis on the Predictive Validity of the Adult Attachment Interview." *Psychological Bulletin* 117, no. 3 (May 1995): 387–403.
7. Ainsworth et al., *Patterns of Attachment*, 32.
8. Ibid., 31.
9. Manuela Veríssimo and Fernanda Salvaterra, "Maternal Secure-Base Scripts and Children's Attachment Security in an Adopted Sample." *Attachment and Human Development* 8, no. 3 (Sept. 2006): 262.

10. Mary Main, "Mary D. Salter Ainsworth: Tribute and Portrait." *Psychoanalytic Inquiry* 19 (1999): 682–776; see 696–97.
11. Mary D. S. Ainsworth and Robert S. Marvin, "On the Shaping of Attachment Theory and Research: An Interview with Mary D. Ainsworth." (Fall 1994) *Monographs of the Society for Research in Child Development*, vol. 60. no. 2/3, *Caregiving, Cultural and Cognitive Perspectives on Secure-Base Behavior and Working Models: New Growing Points of Attachment Theory and Research* (1995): 11.
12. Yvonne Brackbill, "Extinction of the Smiling Response in Infants as a Function of Reinforcement Schedule." *Child Development* 29, no. 1 (March 1958): 115–24.
13. John Keegan, *The Face of Battle* (New York: Penguin Books, 1983).
14. Marina Zelenko, Helena Kraemer, Lynne Huffman, Miriam Gschwendt, Natalie Pageler, and Hans Steiner, "Heart Rate Correlates of Attachment Status in Young Mothers and Their Infants." *Journal of the American Academy of Child and Adolescent Psychiatry* 44, no. 5 (May 2005): 470–76.
15. Main, "Mary D. Salter Ainsworth," 702.
16. D. W. Winnicott, "Communicating and Not Communicating Leading to a Study of Certain Opposites (1963)," in *The Maturational Processes and the Facilitating Environment: Studies in the Theory of Emotional Development* (New York: International Universities Press, 1965), 186.

On Smushing

I wield the power of life and death over thousands daily. I am absently smushing ants as I write this. It's summer, so there are ants in my house, as there are every year, and I have put out ant traps, which have had no effect, as is also traditional, so I'm inefficiently smushing them one by one. I am inconsistent in my enforcement: I'll massacre dozens at a time in a fit of pique after catching them glutting themselves in my sugar bowl, but then, seeing one ant moping around on the counter, looking sort of forlorn and hang-dog, I'll hesitate. He looks like maybe he's not having such a great day already. Getting smushed is the last thing this guy needs. Dispensing death and clemency so capriciously—killing on petulant impulse, granting pardons at whim—gives me an Olympian view of how men must live and die in battle or disasters: one just unlucky, in the wrong place at the wrong moment, while the guy next to him is miraculously spared for no reason at all. *As flies to wanton boys, are we to the gods.*

Ants, as individuals, do not seem like very complicated animals—I'm sure myrmecologist E. O. Wilson would correct me on this—but every time I smush one I am uncomfortably aware I am extinguishing one living being's single chance to be alive for eternity. (Unless you believe in reincarnation: maybe next time I get to be the ant and he gets to smush me.) It's hard to believe Descartes convinced even himself that animals were automata; as I watch an ant scramble frantically to escape my annihilating thumb, he certainly looks every bit as conscious of his own mortality as I am. As an Andy Breckman lyric goes: *Cockroach on the bathroom wall / asshole at the shopping mall . . . Do their best to not get killed.*

In this, as in so many things, my sixteen-year-old self would be disappointed in me. At that age I thought maybe Jainism was the religion for me. All I really knew about the Jainists was that they carried little brooms with them everywhere to sweep insects out of their paths, lest they accidentally step on a single bug. I was a kid who used to spend most of my time at pools rescuing slowly flailing beetles from drowning, so this appealed to me. Though I note that Jainism originated in India, a country to which stinkbugs are not indigenous. The stinkbug, an invasive species, has taken over the mid-Atlantic region in the last few years as swiftly as the Martians conquered England. It was from stinkbugs that I learned that any animal in sufficient numbers, no matter how harmless, can be horrific. An effective stinkbug trap can be constructed out of a two-liter soda bottle and an LED light, but I find it more thorough and meditative to eradicate them through piecework using the nozzle attachment of my vacuum cleaner. They make a very satisfying *thhhhhP!* sound when you suck them up. They then get to live out the rest of their lives in the oubliette of the vacuum bag. Even funner is the handheld bug zapper my neighbor Gene gave me, a plastic tennis racket with an electrified mesh: mosquitoes explode like little TIE fighters when you swat them with it, with a dramatic *SPAKK* of blue-white light. So my compassion is not quite Buddha-like in its embrace.

Mice are a much stickier moral problem. Mice are mammals, and, it has to be admitted when you look at them in the light of day, cute—bright-eyed, wriggly little creatures. You can see why they make such endearing cartoon characters. In an ideal world I would be content to coexist with mice. But my Gandhian live-and-let-live attitude hardens into a more Fleming/McCartney-esque one when I go to enjoy my first cup of coffee of the day and find a tiny blackened turd in my mug. This seems like a deliberate insult, an outlaw's insolent calling card. It is then that I set about carefully daubing the trigger of a mousetrap with peanut butter. So begins a wearisome cycle of vengeance and remorse.

A traditional mousetrap is designed to function like a guillotine, killing instantly and painlessly, but human technology is imperfect. Having to dispose of the limp corpse of a mouse is a depressing enough chore with which to begin the day, but what do you do when you find the mouse alive, maimed and crying on your kitchen counter? Mercy-smush the mouse with a rock? Put it outside and hope it'll recover? It will not. It will die of sepsis under your porch, and smell. Whatever you do, you are condemned to feel like John Wayne Gacy for days. These days I prefer to use clever balance-activated traps that harmlessly capture the mouse. When I catch one I carry the trap out to the car, place it on the passenger seat, and drive it up the road to let it out near the house of my neighbor Gene, who likes animals. Except even these "humane" traps can have horrible unintended consequences: I've accidentally left one set when I was about to leave the house for weeks, and returned to find the pitiful corpse of a mouse inside who'd slowly thirsted to death in the dark.

I feel badly about all this killing to varying degrees, ranging from not one bit (mosquitoes, horseflies) to gut-clenching shame (the mice, the mice). The cartoonist Ruben Bolling once drew a handy chart explaining the ethical hierarchy of living things, from close relatives to plants, rating each YES/NO/SOMETIMES OF IF YOU'RE IN THE MOOD in categories ranging from "Should You Help It?" to "Can You Eat It?" Some of these biases are based on help versus harm (cats and dogs are our pals and protectors, some snakes and mosquitoes can kill us), but some are irrational prejudice. (How come we think of hippos as amusing tutu-wearing buffoons when they kill more people than tigers or rhinos, but fear the giant squid, who never bothered anybody?) It is my official policy never to kill spiders, even though occasionally a large hairy one drops out of the rafters right onto the back of my hand and I must walk swiftly to the door holding my hand as far away from me as it will get, reciting *I must not fear, fear is the mind-killer*, etc. My rationale is: spiders eat insects, and the enemy of my enemy should not be smushed. Yes this is a little like arming the mujahideen, but as far as I'm concerned, mosquitoes and stinkbugs are the Soviet Union, and there's a war on. Plus, anyone who's read *Huck Finn* knows that killing spiders is bad luck.

It's impossible to live and move through this world without killing something. Right now the woolly caterpillars, those harbingers of winter, are undertaking their tragic annual mass migration to the other side of whatever road they're near, and it is just about impossible to avoid running over a few of them while you're out doing errands unless you're willing to risk your own life by swerving last-second to spare them. Just driving the ten minutes to the library and back, I wince as I obliterate butterflies when I fail to brake in time to whip them into the slipstream over the car, or, worse, the occasional lightning bug, whose splattered magical guts leave a fluorescing greenish-gold smear of stars across my windshield that I then have to watch fade heartbreakingly away. Once I struck an indigo bunting who'd been sitting in the road: I just didn't see him in time, and he couldn't fly out of the way of my grille. I stopped and got out and stood watching him die in the grass, slowly spreading his wings, iridescent under the sun. Just one minute ago I stepped out in my lawn and felt something squish under my heel. Inside my slipper I found the body of a daddy longlegs, an animal of which I am rather fond, its attached legs still twitching. I helplessly kill dozens, if not hundreds, of animals daily with my big dumb blundering existence.

It's fastidious and silly in this culture, kind of sissyish, to confess to feeling bad about smushing bugs. As far as we're concerned, bugs are household dirt that moves. I recently read an article about the survivors of an earthquake in the Tibetan city of Jyekundo saving thousands of near-microscopic crustaceans from the mud as an act of devotion. This may seem like a trivial ritual, a waste of time, but it is, at least, more real than posting condolences on Facebook or applying a custom RIP decal to your car's rear window. A bug may be a small, unimportant thing, but maybe killing or saving one isn't. Every time I smush a bug I can feel myself smushing something else, too—repressing an impulse toward mercy, ignoring a little throb of remorse. Maybe it would feel better to decide that killing even a bug matters. Does devaluing tiny insignificant lives have some effect whereby we become more callous about larger, more important ones, like a karmic broken-window theory? People running for cover on the ground must look antlike from a bomber or a drone—as flies to wanton boys. As entrepreneur Harry Lime asks: "Would you really feel any pity if one of those dots stopped moving forever?"

This summer I drove a bag of garbage that was attracting fruit flies (kill without qualm) down to the dumpster at the end of my road. I went to lift up the lid of the dumpster, where what did I see but two wretched-looking raccoons huddled together in the corner, hiding their faces from the light. They couldn't have been in there for too long or they would've roasted to death in the recent heat wave. At least they weren't going hungry: the floor of the dumpster was covered in denuded corncobs, squashed watermelon rinds, and other raccoon amuse-bouches. Still, they looked scrawny and matted and miserable in there; they must've had a bad night of it.

What I had here was a Situation. I put down my bag of garbage and turned off the car. I trotted off to a shed where I found just what was needed—a piece of lumber about six feet long. Raccoons may not grasp the concept of favors or gratitude, but they instantly grasped the concept of the ramp. I hadn't even lowered it to the dumpster's floor before one of them eagerly reached up and grabbed it with his paws. They're extremely clever, dexterous animals; I have no doubt they will be the next species to set paw on the moon if we successfully exterminate ourselves. I set the board down on the edge of the dumpster and backed off fast. They both clambered up it, crawled across the dumpster's rim, and plopped to the ground, then slunk off into the woods whence they'd come to rehydrate, debrief, and generally recollect their dignity. When I told this story to my neighbor Gene, who sets bowls of meat out for the local vultures, he told me that he lets those same raccoons out of the dumpster once a week or so. So okay, maybe I am not a hero in the raccoon community. But whenever I think of all the harm I've done in this world, through cruelty or carelessness or just by the unavoidable crime of being in it, I try to remember how I felt standing there, watching them go.

Orientation

New faculty orientation at Scott College was the first time in adulthood that I've had to worry about not crying in public. It was like that nightmare of being back in high school and having missed out on the first day somehow—already being way behind, not knowing where your locker or homeroom is, a frightened, clueless freshman again. I had not had anything like a real job since the early nineties, and couldn't even figure out how to arrange my face during a meeting; I tried to remember the paying-attention expression that had gotten me through college. It was a crushing deluge of information: several intimidatingly thick packets of material were handed out, including everything from a map of campus to new policies on sexual harassment/assault to the holiday schedule to "What to Do If a Shooter Is Reported on Campus." Someone was explaining the school's incomprehensible sui generis alternating-weeks schedule while I was still trying to imagine what, exactly, I *would* do if a shooter were reported on campus. I mean, who knows what I would really do in this hopefully hypothetical situation? Maybe I'd grab the nearest nineteen-year-old as a human shield and flee, weeping with fear. "They can't tell you to put yourself at risk," my friend Harold, a career educator, explained later. "But if you're any kind of a teacher, you know what you have to do." It's like when a little kid reaches up and takes your hand: whether you even like children or not, you are instantly forced into the role of the grown-up, the guardian. A role is a powerful thing. I hadn't met my students yet—they hadn't even registered for classes, were still theoretical—but on some level I decided, sitting there, that if there ever were a shooter on campus, none of my students was going to get killed before I did. I realized I had totally missed the explanation of the schedule. I would never grasp it.

At a time in my life when writing had become as fulfilling as doing my taxes, and about as remunerative, a colleague had suggested I apply to teach at Scott College for a semester. Two of my ex-girlfriends happened to be alumni of the school, and they were both smart, passionate, moral people who'd made unconventional paths for themselves in life. Although one of them had loved Scott and the other hadn't, they both had an intensely personal relationship with the place that I certainly didn't have with my own alma mater, a tense and joyless institution. Even now, in their thirties, they both still spoke its name with an unselfconscious reverence, told stories about lesbian mariachi serenades and people named Celery who ran all-night sandwich-delivery services for the stoned, and talked about their time there as if they'd once been queens in Narnia.

Scott had historically been a women's college; it had only gone coed in the late '60s, and the female-to-male ratio still ran about 70:30. Several of my friends had subjected me to some comradely mockery about teaching at a predominantly girls' school. "I can't believe you are even pretending you are not going to fuck your students," said Harold, a bad man. Our friends' little jests at our expense are never less hilarious than when they're based on what we like to think are obsolete perceptions, the same way it infuriates you when a sibling condescends to you as though you were still six. I suppose it also rankled because secretly I had some worries myself.

It was true I had historically not shown an iron will in resisting temptation. This was in pursuance of a policy, since modified in practice if not wholly recanted in principle, that you should have as much sex as possible while you're alive. Apparently a guy gets a reputation.

And Scott had a reputation of its own; my alumni friends told me that the artsiest, most eccentric, flamboyantly fucked-up girls from all over America were drawn to Scott, where they vied to outdo one another in artsiness, eccentricity, and flamboyant fucked-uppèdness. My ex-girlfriend Diana, a Scott alumna herself, warned me to prepare myself for "some literally incredible sexual come-ons" from undergraduates. I mentally rehearsed a speech for use in this event—really a very moving speech, I thought, respectful but firm—that I knew I would never actually give. The one time it seemed I might be about to face this situation, when a student suddenly pulled off her sweater in my office, which had several large windows, I did not deploy the speech but instead sat paralyzed, praying, *Oh, please, pretty lady, do not, oh do not.* It turned out she just wanted to show me a tattoo.

This was Gina, who had told me during our initial interview that she got naked in front of people a lot. Another sui generis institution at Scott is that at the beginning of the semester students interview their prospective professors to decide which classes they want to sign up for. Gina said she wanted to try to write because she thought it was unimaginably brave. She was an actress, she explained, a natural exhibitionist, so she had no inhibitions about taking her clothes off in front of an audience. "I was just naked in front of a bunch of people yesterday," she said.

". . . onstage?" I asked, hopefully.

"Nah," she said, "but baring yourself *emotionally*—that's *really* scary." Another prospective student, Becca, told me that she'd always wanted to write, too, but frankly acknowledged that fear was holding her back. I thought about saying something I wasn't sure would be professional, thought better of it, and then said it anyway: "Listen," I told her. "I've never taught this course before. I am terrified to teach it. How about you take the course, I'll teach it, and we'll face our fears together?"

As I'd feared, I turned out to be a conscientious and dedicated teacher. Unfortunately this involved doing a lot of work. I blew a whole day at the New York Public Library tracking down and scanning a modern translation of Montaigne so my students would not have to slog through Elizabethan English and be afflicted with an unfair hatred of Montaigne for life. Editing and commenting on my students' writing took me about an hour per essay. I found myself writing things like *Vern I swear to Christ if you make me correct one more apostrophe—*. After a day of class I would get home and lie on top of my bed with my shoes on for a couple of hours just listening to Marvin Gaye, too tired even for a beer. I could not figure out how to conserve my energies—how to do any less without caring less. Of course I still procrastinated actually grading my students' essays, compared to which getting shot in their defense seemed a self-indulgent daydream.

Veteran teachers will recognize in all this the doomed improvidence of the novice. A colleague at Scott told me, in mid-October, that she hadn't looked at any student writing yet. I was in awe of her sloth. My friend Margot, on hearing how long I took to copyedit a single essay, advised me that I was insane. Five minutes was plenty of time to spend on a student piece, she told me; my job was to improve their writing, not perfect it. She wondered whether I was trying to prove something to myself, or to them. "Are you invested in your students seeing you in a certain way?" she asked. Margot, a journalist, has always had an annoying knack for asking the right question.

A year earlier I'd gotten one of those emails that leaves you embroiled in an imaginary argument for days—angrily defending yourself, composing contemptuous rebuttals, and posing damning rhetorical questions, all while secretly wondering whether it's possible you're the asshole after all. An email you finally delete not just so that you won't be tempted to reread it but to try to make it not have existed.

It was from an ex of mine named Rosalind. Rosalind had been twenty-one at the time we'd gone out, twenty years younger than me. Our involvement, which had lasted for several months, had ended about five years earlier. Since we'd broken up I'd seen her only once, to catch up over drinks, and as far as I'd known we were still on friendly, affectionate terms. I'd written her recently because I'd been thinking of her, with tenderness and regret, wishing I had treated her more carefully.

I am familiar with the so-called campsite rule of intergenerational relationships: that the older partner should leave the younger one in better condition than s/he found him or her. But it sometimes happens that you think you've done your best, take a last look around and everything looks pristine—garbage cleaned up, fire doused—and drive home, and it's not until much later, when you hear about a wildfire in that area that charred thousands of square acres, that you start to wonder whether you're 100 percent certain you extinguished every ember.

Apparently Rosalind, now teaching students the same age she'd been back when we were seeing each other, had had some belated regrets about our liaison. She wasn't claiming it hadn't been consensual or that she hadn't enjoyed it at the time, she said, but now, in retrospect, she felt she'd been taken advantage of. She sent me a link to an article about the development of the female brain, which, according to the studies cited, is not complete until the age of twenty-five. She said that I, as a man, could never presume to understand the phenomenon of "slut-shaming" and how our relationship had degraded her in the eyes of her friends, and in her own. She told me I hadn't respected the boundaries of her current relationship by writing her (she had mentioned she had a boyfriend the last time we'd corresponded); just being in contact with me felt inappropriate. It really wasn't the sort of email you wanted to get. She appended a link to a music video, which presumably reiterated her feelings in song. I did not choose to view it.

Self-castigation is just as suspect as self-justification, and they're both pretty tedious. I could argue in my defense that Rosalind and I were both consenting adults; she was not my student, or my intern, or my employee. And I'd genuinely liked her: she was very smart, funny, and ambitious, and had more depth than I would've expected in someone so young. Although I wouldn't have called her my girlfriend, I also wouldn't have called our relationship an affair or a fling. We had what we called a Thing. We had our restaurant, a neighborhood place in a basement with elderly regulars who'd clearly been coming for decades; we successfully shot off a model rocket, after several frustrating launch anomalies, from a local park; she saw me weep at an amateur performance of *Amahl and the Night Visitors*.

But it could also be argued that this is all bullshit. I knew better than to get involved with Rosalind, and not only because of our age difference. The "depth" I appreciated in her had been gouged out by grief; Rosalind had been orphaned when she was a child, and I, longtime listener of *Loveline*, understood that this had to be one reason she'd be attracted to someone so much older than herself. Like a lot of young women, she was looking for a lot more than sex, but thought of sex as a way to get it. She acted as if she were fine with our casual arrangement, which at first I accepted at face value, both because guys are sort of stupid and literal but also because it was convenient.

Despite my best efforts at denial, I did have a dilapidated conscience that still sputtered to life and gave me trouble once in a while. Eventually I couldn't ignore that Rosalind was more invested in our relationship than I could be, and I resolved to break things off with her. But every time I mentally prepared myself to have the Talk with her, she would wear something low-cut and my will would be vaporized. I'd have to report back to Harold that I had failed to end things yet again, and he would call me a laughingstock, a thing of shame. I started to worry that my involvement with Rosalind would somehow be exposed, and I would be disgraced. "What are you *talking* about?" Harold mocked me. "What's the headline gonna be: **MAN FUCKS WOMAN**?"

Well, it was true there was nothing Pearl-Harbor-newsworthy about a man sleeping with a younger woman. But my irrational fear that our banal involvement would somehow become a public scandal suggested that, on some level, I felt ashamed of it. I finally broke things off with Rosalind as kindly as I could, which is never very kind. She took it about as well as anyone ever does, which is never very well.

Maybe such relationships are always inherently unequal, if only because forty-year-olds can still at least sort of remember what it was like to be twenty, but there is no way for a twenty-year-old to imagine what it's like to be forty. But they're also more complicated and reciprocal than the cynical exploiter/innocent victim narrative wants to allow. Sex is *supposed* to be illicit and transgressive; flouting boundaries of power, age, race, class, etc. is a basic formula of erotic fantasy. (A female friend of mine and I express this principle: "Hot Because It's Wrong.") Both older and younger partners are craving some kind of validation from each other, trying to siphon off some quality they imagine the other possesses. Young people are attracted not just to older people's power or status or accomplishment but to the sense, illusory though it usually is, that we know something that still eludes them, that we're more at ease with ourselves or comfortable in the world. And the young wield more power over their elders than they imagine: we're intimidated by their alien culture, covetous of their luxurious futures, and in thrall to their immaculate bodies, still undefiled by time—witness Rosalind's cleavage blasting my best intentions to shambles.

But we're also hoping to contract from them some of their drunken, impulsive, unprotected passion. I don't fall in love as easily, or as often, in middle age. Even the angst and disillusionment of the young are enviably fresh. Although I don't miss the embarrassing outbreaks of infatuation and heartbreak, I do miss the days when songs like "The Nearness of You" evoked emotions that were still accessible to me. One of the last times I felt that kind of delirium was during a flirtation with a twenty-three-year-old skydiver who made me read Michael Moorcock. My friend Lauren, who's confessed to getting a little giddy around the attractive young herself, feels there's something exploitative about it, though not in the usual moralistic or political sense: it's less sexually predatory than a kind of emotional vampirism. Marx's dictum, "You're only as old as the girl you feel,"* tells an unpresentable truth out of the side of its mouth.

When someone attacks you, your initial reaction is not to examine your conscience; it's to get angry and defensive. For days after getting Rosalind's email I stalked around the city in a black funk, hissing arguments under my breath. It was obvious to me that Rosalind, with the benefit of a few years' perspective and probably some therapy, was revising the narrative of her past, as we all periodically do. But it seemed unreasonable for her to expect me to subscribe to this new version in which I had to play the villain. I thought she was trying to disown any agency and retroactively foist all the blame for our relationship off on me. At what age, exactly, do we start to take responsibility for our own bad decisions? Was I supposed to have ignored what she'd said she wanted at the time

---

* Groucho, not Karl.

and act, instead, based on what I ought to have known she *would* want, years in the future, for her former self? Love and sex are arenas in which we all inevitably get hurt, where our desires collide. *Caveat amator!*

Obviously I should've been composing an apology instead of a defense; I was twenty years older than Rosalind, and should've been able to see past her anger to the hurt beneath it. It's just hard to empathize with someone who hates you. I also should've known better than to wrangle with an ex over whose version of your shared past gets to be the "true" story, but I couldn't help but try to refute her image of me as some predatory old lecher. So, inevitably, I wrote Rosalind back. What, I asked her to clarify, the fuck?

A mistake, of course. "I didn't want to be blunt, and I didn't want to be cruel," she wrote, but now, she said, not really sounding all that sorry about it, she would be. She then presented me with a bouquet of long-hoarded accusations and grievances. She felt not so much used or judged as ashamed, revolted. She still had bad dreams about me—barging into her apartment or parties, humiliating her in front of her friends. "I think you see yourself as some sort of victimized protagonist here," she wrote. "As far I'm concerned, you're *that guy*" (italics hers).

"No one ever wants to accept that they are *that guy*" (her paragraphing also).

I'd once drawn Rosalind a picture of her cat, Ike, ferociously humping a Chinese dragon marionette she owned, which was a thing that Ike would do. Even though Rosalind had specifically commissioned a work of art on this subject, I couldn't help but wonder whether now, in retrospect, she didn't see in it some sordid allegory. In its thought balloon, the ill-used puppet is imagining that it is an actual dragon, vast-winged and terrible, skeletonizing the lecherous cat with one incendiary breath.

I did feel scalded, flayed, by Rosalind's email. It was like seeing a photo of yourself that you immediately want to rip up or delete because it shows some aspect of you—a lined, sagging face, a mushy, shapeless chin—that you don't want to see. Like most people, I like to think of myself as basically kind and well-intentioned. It was disturbing to know I'd become a bogeyman in someone else's imagination. I'd always hated books and movies in which someone is accused of a crime they didn't commit; I could never even stand it when the public thinks Spider-Man is a criminal. All that dread of a false accusation probably masks the fear of a just one. A lot of my self-righteous anger at Rosalind was shame twisted inside out: I was afraid she was telling me something ugly about myself that might be true. No one wants to be *that guy*.

I conferred with my friend Zoey, a polyamorous "pleasure activist" and veteran of many a complex sexual pickle. "That's really upsetting," she said, in sympathy with both Rosalind and me. Her recommendation was that I tell Rosalind I'd been appalled to learn that she now saw our relationship as exploitative, and ask her whether there was anything I could do to undo the damage. I brooded on this advice for a couple of days, distastefully entertaining the idea of behaving decently, loath to let go of the dream of unconditional vindication. Eventually I summoned up or impersonated the best version of myself I could and wrote another email to Rosalind, apologizing for my initial reaction, admitting that I shouldn't have gotten involved with her in the first place, and offering to make whatever amends I could. She didn't write back.

I spent a long time after that, longer than I like to admit, composing emails to Rosalind in my head. Some were conciliatory; some were vindictive. I still wasn't sure whether I regretted getting defensive or apologizing. I vacillated between resentment and shame, between seeing her as a nasty, irrational brat and myself as a big sleazy creep. This is the problem with these he-said, she-said situations: you never know who to believe, not even when one of them is you.

I always wore a suit and tie to class, often with a pocket square, less as a disguise to dupe my students into buying my authority than as a costume to help me get in character, and to armor myself against encroaching feelings of fraudulence. There was a day in class, a few weeks into the semester, when I was either on powerful cold medication or just really sick, that I briefly felt as if I were on LSD, and could not sustain the fiction in my own mind that I belonged in charge. I don't think my external demeanor changed, but secretly I kept wondering: *Why is everyone listening to me? How come* I *get to say who's allowed to talk? I could tell them to read anything—the* Foundation *trilogy,* The 120 Days of Sodom, Bread and Jam for Frances*—and they would have to do it!* Maybe all teachers have these spells of vertiginous insecurity now and then. "Just remember," one of my colleagues had advised me, "you know more than they do."

I tried to be forthright with my students about the fact that I was barely ahead of them, still struggling with the same problems in writing and in life, almost as clueless as they were; I'd just been clueless a little longer. About the only inside information about being an adult I had to impart to them was that there is no such thing; at no point do you learn the big secret, become privy to some wisdom that enables you to move through the world with assurance. Once a student asked me in a conference, in some desperation, whether there was some happy medium between getting married and buying a house in Westchester and running off with the wrong man to live in a shack in the woods—whether there was any balance to be found between stability and passion, sanity and happiness. I worried that I probably ought to have more perspective on this question than a twenty-one-year-old, but about all I could tell her was: Welcome.

Conferences were yet another sui generis institution at Scott: professors were expected to have a half-hour one-on-one meeting with each student every other week to discuss her work. My office was in a building called Twaddell, which also housed dorms—also per some idiosyncratic pedagogical theory, academic and residential buildings at Scott were not separated—so sometimes, ducking into the hall bathroom before class in full professorial drag, I'd bump into a hungover undergrad in her pajamas with a toothbrush and we'd both say, "Uh, hi." The academic and the personal awkwardly crossed paths in conferences as well: because I was teaching the writing of personal essays, at times my role was not as different from that of a therapist or father confessor as I would've liked. I heard myself saying things like "Say more about your father," which were appropriate in context but nonetheless felt weird.

Whether my students at Scott had any more problems than are standard among undergraduates everywhere I don't know, but, because most novice writers assume that the best subject matter is whatever is most traumatic or sensational, I got to hear about them all. They suffered an array of afflictions so endemic among twenty-first-century upscale American adolescent females that you can probably list them yourself. I read, among other things, about cheating fathers, abusive fathers, and absent fathers, about affairs with much older men, and girls convincing themselves they were cool with things they were not in fact cool with. It isn't easy to be anyone in this world, but, thanks to the privileged window I was given into the lives of my students at Scott, I can tell you this: it is harder to be a girl.

Sometimes a student's prose and structure were accomplished enough that I got to welcome her to the more advanced and intractable problems of writing. I'd have to break it to her, as gently as possible, that a lover's betrayal, a parent's abandonment, even the death of a friend, are all banal clichés to that heartless bastard the Reader unless you can somehow compel or beguile him into caring. I'd urge her to "go back in for the snakes"—an idiom derived from a scene in *Pee-wee's Big Adventure*, meaning to plunge back into an essay to grasp the thing she'd been trying to avoid and bring it up, slithery and wriggling, into the light. Sometimes I'd decide we weren't going to figure it out sitting down in my office, and we'd have to step outside and pace around on the lawn for a while, both of us thinking hard, occasionally pausing as we crossed paths to run some half-formed idea by the other, two writers at work.

It was an intimate business, teaching—as intimate as my writing this, or as your reading it. I was asking my students to entrust me with the tenderest, most painful stories of their lives, to share their most unattractive emotions, heterodox thoughts, and uncool opinions, playing surrogate for the ideal reader they might one day be brave enough to confide in. Gina was right: showing someone a rough draft is more terrifying than being naked in front of them. What with this intense, ambiguous mix of authority and trust, submission and power, baring oneself for someone else's approval, dispensing admonitions and clemency, conferring in confidence about the most personal things, it's no wonder so many teachers and students, mentors and protégés, end up falling in love, or at least into bed.

I'd spent my first few days on the Scott campus trying to cultivate a Zen-like detachment from the allurements of the flesh—or, failing that, to self-administer a kind of mental Ludovico Technique whereby I would instantly quash any libidinous ideation by imagining the hideous public disgrace that would ensue if any of it were to leak into reality. But once I'd started teaching I found, to my relief, that none of this stringent conditioning was necessary. Out of a class of sixteen, fourteen of my students were female, and although, yes, yes, they were lovely young women, I told my friends, *No* seriously *dudes*, no prurient thoughts regarding them ever oozed into my mind. It just wasn't like that: they were just so young, still so unformed; far fewer years separated them from a serious interest in Nickelodeon than from me.

Several of my female friends assured me that some of my students must have had crushes on me, but I had a hard time believing that they even saw me as belonging to the same species as themselves, or inhabiting the same seething sexual universe. The skewed gender demographic at Scott played havoc with the normal codes and mores of mating. "It's not natural," my student Becca complained. "It's like the army!" Fiona once asked me in conference: "Do you know the phrase we have at Scott—'The Golden Cock'?" Fiona was a quietly lovely young woman with whom you could have an intelligent, adult conversation. I may have had to close my eyes as I answered her. "No, Fiona," I said. "I do not." This idiom turned out to refer to the phenomenon whereby a Scott male of no more than ordinary sexual street value becomes, by virtue of the economics of artificial scarcity, such a hotly sought-after commodity that he comes to believe he possesses . . . the you-know-what. This syndrome can so thoroughly derange a young man's estimation of his own desirability that he will dump someone like Fiona. (I could only imagine the brutal devaluation that awaited these boys when they were returned to the unregulated market.) My friend Diana confirmed that this distorted sense of limitless sexual possibility had permanently disfigured the personalities of some of the boys she'd known there: they'd run amok like junkies in a pharmacy and rendered themselves forever unfit for real relationships.*

When I reminded Fiona that there were qualified counselors on

---

* It did occur to me to wonder, too late, why I hadn't figured this factor into my own college application strategy: Why hadn't *I* gone to a 70 percent female college where I could've disported myself like a satyr?

campus, one of whom I wasn't, she told me she knew that; she just needed to run her situation by an adult. "Did you find one?" I joked feebly. Fiona, who did not know that I was then living in a friend's basement and $400 overdrawn, didn't laugh. One thing that working with young people impresses upon you is that, whatever age you may feel inside, you are no longer young.

Time to go back for the snakes: it still took me aback—both flattered and wounded me—when a student held a door for me or called me "sir." To me they looked like pretty girls; to them I looked like one of their dad's friends. For someone like me, who'd never married or had children, gotten a mortgage or even a credit card—any of the inglorious trophies that mark the graduation from youth to middle age—it had been easy to convince myself that, past a certain developmental threshold, we were all just grown-ups. Which is how I could feel it was fine for me to date Rosalind. But a friend of mine, long married and the father of a young daughter, once told me that, although of course he still noticed women in their twenties, the thought of hitting on one of them just seemed "grotesque." I remembered an article about a high school teacher who'd been convicted of having sex with several of his underage students, in which friends and colleagues were quoted as saying that he'd always thought of himself as one of them, a young person himself. Thinking of that story now, I saw him as less predatory than stunted, pathetic.

My own personality had felt continuous since college: I still felt like my same clueless goofball twenty-year-old self and still cringed and damned myself over his fuckups and derelictions. But I could see that my students were just kids, still halfway adolescent and, despite their sophisticated sex lives and substance abuse, more blameless than they knew. Their essays about getting wasted and fucking their ex's best friend failed to appall me with their depravity. I wanted to tell them that they barely had free will yet; they were still acting out on impulses whose origins they didn't understand.

And I found I could begin to make the same allowances for my own young self that I did for them. One student, remembering with shame how she'd avoided her mother after she was diagnosed with cancer, asked me, "Who *does* that?" I thought of my own father's terminal illness and told her: "Everyone."

Maybe my initial feelings of fraudulence were protecting me from an even more unpleasant insight: that I belonged in charge after all. What if what little I knew about life now was all there was to know? When a student asked me, in all naked earnestness, how to go from being someone like him to someone like me—by which he seemed to mean encyclopedically erudite—I thought of one of my own old professors, whose study looked like a supervillain's lair and is still featured on lists of the world's greatest libraries, and I wanted to tell him, *No,* those *were the* real *grown-ups.* But maybe there had never been any grown-ups.

Toward the end of the semester, one of my students had a serious crisis—the grown-up, real-world, life-and-death kind. When she stayed behind after class to confide in me, I said, "Oh, you poor girl," and hugged her. I offered to take her out for banana walnut pancakes. I didn't know what to do. A colleague gave me some hard-earned advice about not getting too enmeshed in my students' personal problems, which, he assured me, would be serious, legion, and insoluble; he'd had to adopt a firm, dispassionate policy of compartmentalization for the sake of his own home life. Another colleague warned me never to hug a student again for any reason: professors had been charged under Title IX for inappropriate eye contact. At least I forbade her to read one more page of David Foster Wallace's *Oblivion*, her current reading-for-pleasure pick, and prescribed instead William Goldman's abridgement of *The Princess Bride,* S. Morgenstern's immortal tale of true love and high adventure. Over Thanksgiving break she reported it was "better than Zoloft."

Although I'd entered into this job apprehensive of temptation and feebly determined to resist it, it wasn't until I'd actually taught for a semester that I understood that I could no more fuck one of my own students than I could strangle my own cat. And it wasn't, for me at least, for the official reasons. The Rules had certainly never prevented me from doing whatever the hell I'd wanted before. And though I know it's counterrevolutionary to say so, I don't believe that all intergenerational relationships are necessarily victim/predator morality plays that inevitably lead to lifelong trauma/well-deserved ruin. The power imbalance between teacher and student is a reasonable objection to relationships between them, but for me it wasn't the only one. As far as I was concerned, the prohibition wasn't only for my students' sakes.

I found I loved the boundaries imposed by my role. In my experience, sexual relationships had seldom led to anything but bitterness, recriminations, and regret; it was a relief to know that the worst I could do to these young women was to publicly shame them over apostrophes or maybe give them a B. My job was to tend to their minds, to make them think hard about the most important things in life, to teach them the low showman's tricks of rhetoric and the music of euphony. I had been placed in what used to be called a position of trust. My students' as-yet-unsmushed love of reading and their yearning, painful as lust, to stretch their abilities far enough to touch their ambitions were as moving to me as children's awe of squirrels or tar bubbles is to their parents. I felt less as though they were being protected from me than that I was. I could understand, in principle at least, why priests are required to be celibate: when you don't want anything from someone, you can give of yourself freely, without fear. I liked being in a position for the first time in which I could actually help someone, dispense advice and encouragement, be generous without an agenda. Where I had the power to be kind.

But, oh, how they *vexed* me, my Scott girls! How they tested me! How I bitched and fretted over them. Arianna kept oversleeping and handing her assignments in late, pleading medication changes and deadline anxiety. Carly kept trying to ingratiate herself with me by finking on her classmates. Idiopathic maladies, family emergencies, and computer trouble proliferated as end-of-semester due dates approached. I formulated a theory to account for Isabel's in-class comments, which seemed to pertain to a very similar, but not identical, discussion taking place in a class much like our own in an adjacent dimension, a theory corroborated when she came to class wearing marijuana-leaf-print pants.

"You love them," Diana taunted me fondly. "I can't take it. It makes me so happy, seeing you become a teacher. It's my favorite thing in life right now."

On the last day of class I invited a friend of mine to guest lecture, and so for the first time all semester I was able to look around the seminar table at the faces of my students without having to think hard about how to respond to a comment, segue to the next point, or subtly nudge us back on topic. And I found that they were very dear to me, those faces, in the same way that the faces of your traveling companions in a foreign country can come to feel as intensely familiar as those of childhood friends after only a few days. I was really very fond of them all, even—maybe especially—the ones who'd most exasperated me. When Gina pulled off her sweater with a theatrical stretch to reveal she was wearing only long underwear beneath it, I silently applauded, the way you do when a beloved sitcom character delivers her signature catchphrase.

Toward the end of the semester, I stuck a little pink Post-it note to my laptop to keep track of which of my students had sent in their final assignments. Eventually it was crammed, in my hurried cursive, with every name in the class. That faded and dog-eared sticker clung there for months after class had ended, just below the keyboard, where the ball of my thumb pressed the bent corner flatter and smudged the pencil fainter whenever I typed. It wasn't some sentimental keepsake or anything; I just kept not taking it off, the way you might leave a ski tag or museum sticker on your coat. Sometime near the end of the winter I found it on the floor near my desk. It had fallen off unnoticed, like a scab flaking from a newly healed wound.

People seldom make a conscious decision to change and then actually follow through and do it. I never do, anyway. If it happens at all, it happens without my noticing; I look back at something I did five or ten years ago and am surprised to realize that I simply wouldn't do it now. That I'm not *that guy* anymore. Not long ago I was telling a friend about one of my students' final essays with what must've been audible adoration, because she interrupted to ask: "Do you love her?" I was actually scandalized. "You mean am I *in love* with her?" I asked. "No! Of course not—she's, like, nineteen! She's my *student*."

Still, don't let's read this as some morality tale of redemption through responsibility—*The Temptations of Timothy; or, a Roué Reformed*. I don't know what redemption even means, and still maintain that responsibility is best delegated to those too slow-witted to avoid it. (I'm also hesitant to give myself too much credit, since virtue comes more easily with age and the ebbing of desire. I've always admired Montaigne for declining to repent of his vices: "I would be ashamed and jealous if the wretched lot of my decrepitude were to be preferred above the years when I was healthy, aroused and vigorous.") The last thing I'd want to be accused of is "growing up"; this is how boring conventional people congratulate you when your spirit breaks. My current girlfriend is, by any standard, old enough to make her own questionable decisions, but still young enough that our relationship is respectably scandalous.

But I am glad to have found, if only for a semester, one human arena in which I could exercise a form of devotion safely firewalled off from desire. A form, really, of love. For what else would you call it, what else could it be that would drive a man to comment in such exhaustive detail on all those essays, to run off all those copies and correct countless apostrophes for what must've averaged out to the hourly wage of a Bangladeshi garment worker? They'll be dispersing into the world soon, my students, to become grad students, librarians, or teachers, some of them maybe even writers, my intellectual and artistic foster daughters. When a student of mine got an essay she'd written in my class published, I was far happier than when I publish anything myself. Late in a life largely given over to hedonism, I had discovered a novel pleasure: being proud of someone. In a sense other than she intended, the answer to my friend's question—"Do you love her?"—was: of course.

Teaching was not some sort of karmic atonement or reparation for Rosalind. The two situations are not analogous. But I sometimes think of the two episodes as speaking of two poles of my character. It frankly makes me uncomfortable to write about them both in the same essay: these parts of us are supposed to be kept sequestered in separate worlds that never touch, like your résumé and your porn. I wonder whether talking about these two things together—the kind of love my friend asked about and the kind I actually felt—makes us so squeamish because the latter is a highly refined, almost unrecognizable form of the former. But it's only politicians, journalists, and other moralists who need to reduce things to Jekyll-and-Hyde terms. Personality isn't a point but a spectrum. Rosalind wanted me to admit that I was an exploitative creep, while I was trying to convince us both that I was really a decent guy; we were both buying into the fallacy that I must be one or the other. The nice guys and the creepy guys are all the same guys.

The trick would be to reconcile these estranged selves—the selfish and the generous, the lecherous and the kind. Ideally, in romantic relationships, desiring someone and caring about her are supposed to coincide. I won't go so far as to say that the two are fundamentally at odds, but they certainly tend to complicate each other. ("Not one couple in a century has that chance," S. Morgenstern writes of true love, "no matter what the storybooks say . . .") Long-married friends tell me that the more truly you know someone, the more important they become to you, the more terrifying the prospect of revealing yourself before them becomes. Getting naked with some stranger is easy; but, like Gina said, "baring yourself *emotionally*—that's *really* scary." How *do* you balance sanity and happiness? About love and sex I still feel almost as clueless as I did at orientation.

There was an afternoon, months after I'd broken things off with Rosalind, when I was biking down Fifth Avenue, wearing a helmet and sunglasses, and I was about to slip past a bus that had pulled over, when I saw a girl about to step off the curb to board. She paused and drew back when she saw me approaching but, seeing that I was braking for her, she gave me a tentative thumbs-up to say *Thanks* or *Good bike etiquette, dude.* She looked tired, at the end of a long day. It was no big deal—just a fleeting instant of civility between two strangers. It took me a few seconds to recognize her out of context, so it wasn't until after she'd stepped on board that I realized that the woman in front of me had been Rosalind. Two former lovers, nearly colliding at rush hour in this city of eight millions. I wanted to say something to her, but it was too late, and Rosalind never knew it was me.

The Uncertainty Principle

I did not have some naïve idea that Diana could save me, in the religious sense or any other. But I'd lately been doing some reading and thinking about the big insoluble questions, and it's possible that modulating my twentieth-century hard-line atheism had left me more open to getting involved with someone who believed in God. And Diana did more than just believe in God; she was actually a pastor.

That's how she answered when people in New York City, capital of Godless East Coast liberal-elite America, asked her what she did: "I'm a pastor, actually." She had started her own church in the heart of hipster Brooklyn, with an unconventional worship service she'd designed herself. But it wasn't some New Agey church where they kept the God talk to a minimum; it was part of a stodgy, respectable, five-hundred-year-old denomination, and although some of her congregants were young people who worked in the arts or for nonprofits, there were also single parents and retirees, the unemployed and the homeless. She was something of a rising star in the clerical world—a charismatic woman who'd created a new church that was attracting young people and growing at a time when the denomination's membership was aging and churches were closing down.

It did not, however, make her a hot commodity on OkCupid. A lot of guys either assumed she must be priggish and virginal, or else fetishized her profession. It must have been a little like being East Asian—having to gauge whether men actually like you or just want to act out some *Madame Butterfly/hentai* fantasy. I suspected the sorts of guys who got off on cassocks and wimples had probably grown up in guilt-inflicting religions that veil sex in secrecy and shame. (These religions never seem to realize that secrecy and shame are the psychological equivalents of thongs and garters.) I told Diana that I associated church with doughy women in print dresses and hairnets, and did not ever need to see her in her clerical collar if we could help it.

For years I'd told people the worst thing about my own religious upbringing was that it was boring. This was meant as a backhanded compliment; it hadn't warped my sexuality, given me nightmares, or left my personality twisted with resentment or shame (let alone withheld medical treatment, subjected me to regular rape, or any other more overt crimes). The values it taught—simple living, service, pacifism—still seemed to me like sane and decent ones. Church was boring, make no mistake—the drawings I did in bulletins could fill a multivolume set of notebooks—but at least it wasted fewer hours of my life than school.

The thing I really couldn't forgive it for was not being true. As a child I'd read picture books about the Good Samaritan, mounted puppet shows about Lot's wife, and listened to children's rock operas about Shadrach, Meshach, and Abednego (*Abednego? Yes, Abednego! Oh, no!*). I'd grown up drawing crayon pictures of Captain America, Prune Face, Jesus, and Frankenstein, all of them more or less equally real to me. In early adolescence, I remembered how the grown-ups had gradually let me in on the secret of Santa Claus, and I kept waiting, increasingly uneasily, for them to do the same thing with God. I can still remember how it felt to lose the easy belief of childhood, and trying to cling to it; the closest thing I can compare it to in adulthood is trying to recapture the feeling you once had for a favorite song, or for someone you're no longer in love with.

What really did God in for me was the reading: Carl Sagan was the kindly uncle who drew me in with a sense of wonder and then gently broke it to me that there was no reason to posit God as first cause; Freud the strict, no-nonsense grandpapa who scoffed that it was all a lot of infantile projection, a big bearded father figure in the clouds; and Nietzsche the disreputable friend of the family who slyly pointed out how religion (and its rebranding, idealism) exalted the purely imaginary over life, the world, or anything real. The Church was probably smart, from a self-serving point of view, to oppose translating the Bible into the vernacular for so long.

Ceasing to believe what your parents and all the other nicest grown-ups you know have always taught you, and still believe themselves, is initially liberating, but it's also alienating. It makes you feel secretly snobby, and sorry, and alone.

Like a lot of unhappy people, I'd formed a half-conscious assumption that depression was a function of intelligence, that happy people just hadn't Realized yet. But after thirty years of smug unhappiness, it was starting to lose some of its adolescent cool. I was drawn to Diana partly because she seemed so effortlessly happy. She showed up last-minute to an animated *Batman* film, threw herself into the seat next to me all flushed and out of breath, and said, "This is going to be awesome." It was this—her certainty that *this was going to be awesome*—that appealed to me. She would wake up in the morning and say, "Today's going to be great." Most mornings I woke up and thought: *Fuck*—this *again*. Of course her happiness wasn't effortless; I knew so little about the condition that I assumed, like all ignorant amateurs watching a disciplined artist or athlete, that it must come easily to her. My agent, attempting to foist off on me some piece of book-party swag, a little journal bound in orange faux leather imprinted with the gilt slogan LIFE IS BEAUTIFUL, suggested that maybe Diana would like it. "Lea," I said, "she's religious, not retarded."

On one of our first dates, when Diana was feeling out whether "the whole pastor thing" was going to be an issue for me, I ventured a potentially impolitic analogy: I told her that I had a friend who was a prostitute, and that her being a pastor signified about as much to me as Zoey's being a whore; it was an unusual occupation that suggested she must be an interesting, unconventional person, but in general I didn't take all that much interest in people's jobs. To my relief, Diana liked this analogy a lot.

In an unfallen world, I suppose, there'd be no need for either prostitution or religion, but both institutions apparently answer basic, insatiable human needs, and I expect they'll both endure for as long as this unfinished, half-crippled species exists. A cynic might say that, of the two rackets, prostitution at least delivers on what it promises. But both Zoey and Diana are exceptions among their respective professions: Zoey sees prostitution as intimate, even loving; Diana once said, "I believe sex is sacred, even if it's with someone you've never met before." They both use the word *vocation* to describe what they do. Zoey says her work fulfills deep needs that aren't being met in any other way; Diana describes her job as creating a space in which people can "become who God meant them to be." Let's not overstrain this analogy—Diana counsels the homeless and lonely and Zoey fucks people with strap-ons—but they're both trying, in very different ways, to help people become themselves.

> What I relate is the history of the next two centuries. I describe what is coming, what can no longer come differently: the advent of nihilism. . . . For some time now our whole

> European culture has been moving as toward a catastrophe, with a tortured tension that is growing from decade to decade: restlessly, violently, headlong, like a river that wants to reach the end . . .

> . . . [W]hen truth enters into a fight with the lies of millennia, we shall have upheavals, a convulsion of earthquakes, a moving of mountains and valleys, the like of which has never been dreamed of. . . . [T]here will be wars the like of which have never yet been seen on earth.

These passages by badly lapsed Lutheran Friedrich Nietzsche have been spooking readers for a century now, and will likely spook them for a century more. (The first is from his notes, posthumously scavenged and published as *The Will to Power*; the second from *Ecce Homo.*) Whence he pulled that "two centuries" figure is anyone's guess, but so far, halfway through his predicted interregnum, it's hard to argue he was wrong: the wars of the twentieth century have made all the previous wars in history look like provincial skirmishes. The greatest of these slaughters were perpetrated in the name of atheistic ideologies (although some of this unprecedented violence can be credited to exciting new breakthroughs in person-killing technology; it's not pleasant to picture what would've happened if the Crusaders had had nerve gas, or the Hittites had Gatling guns). Some people think we're now in the midst of a global religious war between Fundamentalist Islam, still dangerously fervid in its belief, and the dissolute secular West. (Or maybe it's really between Fundamentalist Islam and Fundamentalist Christianity—what the media calls "sectarian violence" when it doesn't involve our sect.) Pluralist societies are recoiling from an influx of Muslim refugees now that *Allahu Akbar* is translated, throughout much of the West, as *Fire in the hole!* Democracies are electing racist reactionaries, longing for another Charles "the Hammer" Martel to drive back the Mohammedan horde. But fundamentalism isn't a sign of a faith's health and strength; it arises in reaction to a faith being fragile, endangered.

I recently attended the deconsecration of a church with my mother. It was a lovely little picture-book country church with a view of rolling northern Maryland pastures where horses grazed. Although I'd never attended this church myself, my mother had been an elder there, my father was buried in its cemetery, and I'd walked my sister down its aisle. After my mother spoke, I snuck out to go sit and read *As I Lay Dying* on a bench beside my father's grave, which was still less depressing than a deconsecration. Mom herself was stoic about the end of the congregation; it was a decade overdue, she said. There were fewer than twenty people still regularly attending, and no one was under eighty-five.

There'll be more and more of these ceremonies in the years to come. A lot of churches are now demographically divided over issues like homosexual clergy and marriage, splitting into younger, urban, progressive churches and older, rural, conservative ones, the former unrecognizable to older church members as the same religion they grew up in, the latter gradually dying off. My mother, in her late seventies, tells me her friends are puzzled and saddened that their children have rejected the faith they were raised in. Mom, who has a master's in theology, is more philosophical, saying that I seem to have internalized the values of the church, if not the metaphysics. Apparently Mom got a lot of shit from her fellow churchgoers over a letter I'd written to our denomination's national magazine in which I outed myself as an atheist but also piously reminded them all of Jesus' line about camels and the eye of a needle.*

---

* For readers who did not regularly attend Sunday school: "It is easier for a camel to go through the eye of a needle, than for a rich man to enter into the kingdom of God." —Matthew 19:24. People who would like to call

On our second date, Diana and I had a tentative talk to determine whether either of us was adamant enough about either Christianity or atheism for this to be what they call, in dating, a deal breaker. I asked Diana what about religion was so important to her. She said it had to do with fostering a sense of community, with the holiness of human connection. She'd deliberately designed her church's service to feel homey, familial. "There are many moments when I wonder if believing in God is silly or foolish or self-serving," she wrote me later, "and then I go to church and eat some bread with some people I've never met and talk about parasites and there is nothing holier." I thought of the semiweekly hootenannies my friends in South Baltimore had had for years, where we'd all gather in the back room of Cox's Pub and play "Roller Derby Queen" and "Bad, Bad Leroy Brown" and talk seriously about women and politics and whether Lando Calrissian could ever truly be trusted again, all while drinking pitchers of beer and the occasional round of shots, toasting: "Gentlemen, our lives are unbelievably great." I said to Diana: "Those things are really important to me, too."

I grew up during a bizarre discontinuity in human history, the second half of the twentieth century, not only post-Nietzsche/Darwin/Freud but also postwar/Holocaust/Bomb. The intellectual and artistic zeitgeist was characterized by what you might call an exalted bleakness: Camus, Beckett, Bacon, Bergman. It was intoxicating stuff for an adolescent to ingest after the stuffy atmosphere of church—intoxicating in the sense of being liberating and stimulating but also, in the long term, poisonous. (I started drinking around the same time.) And yet it wasn't entirely discontinuous with the aesthetics and sensibilities of the iconoclastic northern

themselves Christians but also own Audis and plasma flat screens favor a nuanced interpretation of this aphorism.

European sect I grew up in. The art I loved in adolescence, from Edward Albee to Stanley Kubrick, had a certain hardassed austerity to it, a beauty that wasn't pretty, one that consisted in rigor and renunciation—the renunciation of comforting delusions, the worship of unlovely truth.

Nietzsche was a preacher's kid. His father, a Lutheran pastor, died when Friedrich was five. Preacher's kids have a reputation as troublemakers. Most of them just go wild in their teens and sleep around or get hooked on coke or total the family car, but Nietzsche, who started out as such a nice boy—a chair in philosophy at age twenty-four!—rebelled in a way that the most nihilistic punks and junkies can only envy: by single-handedly trashing a four-thousand-year-old religion. (Is it belaboring the Freudian obvious to point out that someone who'd lost a father in childhood grew up to herald the death of God?) I suspect that when he writes about the tragic irony of the Judeo-Christian virtue of Truth being that religion's ultimate undoing, the entire intellectual tradition self-destructing of its own internal logic, he's writing not just cultural history but autobiography.

I've noticed a qualitative difference between the atheism of people who weren't brought up in a faith and those who underwent an adolescent disillusionment. My friend Lauren's parents were atheists who never took her to church as a child, and her atheism has a placid, matter-of-fact quality that's very different in affect from the passionate, strident atheism of those of us who abandoned their faith. A lot of the latter type tend to be bitter and evangelical in their unbelief: it's like the difference between people who just don't get why alcohol is supposed to be fun and people who had to go to rehab, and now treat wine like cyanide. Although Lauren doesn't love the idea of dying any more than the next person, it doesn't especially upset her to believe that life is meaningless or the universe indifferent. She thinks people like me, who were taught as children that a just and loving God is watching over the sparrows, feel bereft, cheated of something promised. Which is why we're the ones who suffer these chronic cases of existential despair.

In a cardboard box of my own juvenilia that my mother gave me when she moved out of our old house, among the biblical dittos and construction-paper Christs in cotton-ball clouds, I found a sort of heraldic cardboard badge I'd brought home from the Lutheran nursery school I attended. It was suspended by two holes from a piece of yarn, as if meant to be hung from the wall, or maybe worn as a medallion. Its cryptic sigil was a blue shield bearing a weeping silver scallop shell,* with the motto inscribed in Elmer's glue and glitter: "I AM GOD'S CHILD." What are you supposed to do with such a thing? How can you throw that out? I hung it up over my desk, less in the spirit of putting up a crucifix than of framing an X-ray.

It's not so easy to discard a childhood religion. Religion is tenacious, like recessive genes or herpes. It secretly weirds me out that even my Jewish friends who are atheists take for granted that they'll have unnecessary surgery performed on their infants' genitals. You'd think it would be easier to shake off Christianity than Judaism, since it's a creed, not an ethnicity; in theory, if you stop believing it, you stop being one. It turns out to be more complicated. A girlfriend of mine, who'd been brought up working-class Catholic and was a Wiccan by the time I met her, confessed to me years later that she'd returned to the Church. To me it had always seemed as if she'd changed the content of her belief but not the form: Wicca, like Catholicism, was ritualistic, theatrical, full of props and ornament and incantations. Back when I dated her she owned a dagger, which

---

* Research reveals that the scallop shell is a symbol of baptism, which the water droplets would seem to confirm. Is it possible they secretly baptized us at preschool?

she assured me was purely ceremonial. People who convert from brawler to jihadi, or from Klansman to abortion clinic bomber, haven't really switched sides at all; they're just assholes who've changed denominations.

It's less easy for me to see the deeper continuities between my own religious upbringing and my adult intellectual life. I wasn't fucked up by castrating guilt or S and M fantasies of divinely sanctioned torture in the afterlife, like the children of some Catholics or evangelicals, who later have to become Satanists or witches to exorcise their depraved faiths. But I know there are things like that old cardboard badge still hanging up in my own head that I no longer notice, or just haven't had the heart to get rid of. I still cherish certain unexamined delusions of which the world is relentlessly divesting me: that speaking the truth matters; that there is, or ought to be, such a thing as justice; that my actions are observed and some ledger kept of my moral choices; that there are such things as forgiveness and redemption; and, perhaps most pernicious of all, that everything will turn out all right in the end. Regardless of their specific creeds, all religious beliefs presuppose, more invisibly, that there is some objective meaning in the world and a purpose to our lives. Even when a belief system collapses, its underlying presumptions remain, still shaping the space of what it's possible to imagine, like an empty frame.

I remember seeing, on a road trip with my friend Annie, a bumper sticker in a parking lot that read, in stark white-on-black letters: IMAGINE A WORLD WITHOUT GOD. "What a terrible world that would be!" I said to Annie. "Think of it!—it would be a kind of . . . of *nightmare* world! Injustice would go unpunished—power would triumph over virtue—the innocent would suffer, while the greedy and cruel would live lives of luxury!" It got more blackly hilarious the more I thought about it. "Why, life would be without meaning! It would be a . . . a hell on earth!" I reeled around the parking lot and toppled against a car, I was laughing so hard. Annie got it, but it didn't exactly slay her. (Annie wasn't raised religiously, either.) Theodicy, the whole "Problem of Evil" that has stumped theologians and philosophers for millennia—somehow reconciling God's benevolence and omnipotence with tsunamis, melanomas, and Nazis—becomes about as impenetrable as a maze on a kids' menu once you're willing to posit that maybe no one's minding the store. Atheism is simply a more parsimonious theory. It's just not what you'd call a consolation.

My atheism was most impassioned, as most things are, in my twenties. This was around the same time that I read everything Nietzsche wrote. (Nietzsche is like the Hardy Boys for brooding intellectual guys in their twenties, as Ayn Rand is the Nancy Drew of certain brainy, ambitious college girls.) I stayed away from church like a vampire. I can remember the first Easter I declined to join my family at Sunday morning services: I sat naked out on my porch after a shower, letting the sun dry me off, unbaptizing myself. Still, it never occurred to me to proselytize on behalf of my unbelief: Why spread the Bad News? I'd renounced religion, but I was still a practitioner of politeness, and it seemed tacky and mean to go around telling people there was no God, like exposing the Santa hoax to toddlers. When a friend invited me to go with her to an Atheists' March on Washington, I imagined carrying a blank sign.

I did draw a few cartoons on the subject, like "Jesus vs. Jeezus" (the fierce-eyed desert prophet contrasted with a blow-dried American Christ bearing his traditional attributes, the flag and the gun) and "Science vs. Norse Mythology" (illustrating comparative theories of cosmogony and anthropogenesis). Christians, grown lazy and complacent, didn't bother to complain, but the latter aroused the wrath of some followers of Asatru, which is what its adherents call the Norse religion today. They didn't exactly issue a fatwa, but it still gave me pause, since the Vikings were historically not a peace-loving people and I do live right on the water.

You could argue that people lose faith in adolescence because their understanding of God is a childish understanding, literal and concrete, Freud's big omnipotent Dad. (I've often wondered how closely people's conceptions of God—as hardassed disciplinarian or forgiving confidant—or their ideal form of government—law-and-order authoritarianism versus safety-net nanny state—correspond to their own upbringings.) Fundamentalists are people who in adulthood still think as concretely as children: they can grasp symbols, not abstractions; flags and crosses, not ideologies or metaphysics. I'm afraid I'm a fundamentalist at heart; I'm just one who doesn't believe. I envy religious people their sense of meaning and purpose in life, but utility isn't enough of an argument. I've always loved the story Flannery O'Connor, a Southern Catholic, told about being at a New York literary event where Mary McCarthy remarked that the miracle of transubstantiation was a serviceable symbol. O'Connor said, "Well, if it's a symbol, to hell with it." In some perverse way, I almost have less respect for people who say "I'm not religious, but I'm a very *spiritual* person" and believe in a nebulous Something than I do for Southern Baptist dingbats who stand picketing outside abortion clinics. Which is not to say I would prefer to hang out with the latter; only that they actually appear to believe in something, and to act on their convictions. Catholics who are both anti-abortion and anti–death penalty are at least, unlike most liberals or conservatives, consistent. Religion should be transformative; it probably ought to make you a radical, a maniac. If I ever do take up religion again I certainly won't be telling people I believe in Something; I'll be out on the sidewalk with a sandwich board, yelling at people to repent and condemning them all to hell.

A friend told me once she'd have liked to be a fly on the wall for my theological conversations with Diana, but the truth is the subject just never came up much between us. Whenever we did discuss some aspect of belief or creed, it always turned out that we were more or less in agreement. We shared the same un-American Sermon on the Mount politics, though Diana actually went to community meetings and protests and got herself arrested, whereas my own activism took the form of complaining over drinks. When I asked her whether it wasn't at least some part of her job to try to get people to behave more decently, she said, "Not really." She asked me once whether I believed in an afterlife, and I admitted, reluctantly, that I didn't. "I don't think I do, either," she said. I'd always associated faith with certitude and rules, but she seemed to feel that it had less to do with belief than doubt, and wasn't about laws but freedom. Hers was what I would call a theology of uncertainty: she thought that God was in those moments where we feel most ethically squirmy and unsure of ourselves.

We kept threatening to have what we called the Jesus Conversation, but we never got around to it. I did sometimes wonder, looking at all the books on theology and church history stacked around her apartment: So, why Christianity, exactly? Did she really believe all this stuff—the Resurrection, the Virgin Birth, the whole Son of God thing? What about that weird incident with the fig tree? But relationships offer so many spontaneous opportunities for dumb arguments and conflicts that I think neither of us could see any reason to bring it up. And anyway, what people believe is a lot less important or interesting to me than who they are, and what they love. My friend Skelly and I argued about religion over beers for years, but the gulf between our beliefs seemed less divisive than his inexplicable allegiance to Busch.

I would've told you that the things I loved about Diana were irrelevant to her faith, although she probably would've said they were integral to it: her nonjudgmental understanding, her kindness, her high seriousness and deep joy. She saw some beavers the first time she visited my cabin and became obsessed with beavers for months thereafter—their lodges, their teeth, their instinctive hatred of the sound of running water. She would make a beaver face that I had to beg her not to make. There was a day when she had to stand by the side of a dirt road making small talk with a man named Pappy while I was bent over the back seat of my car attempting to wrestle a spare tire out of the back—wildly flailing around, giving up and going limp for a while, then wildly flailing again with renewed frenzy—"like a trapped bug," as she later described it, red-faced and weeping with laughter. Sitting outside one summer night, watching a slow-approaching thunderstorm over the hills, she started crying, and when I asked her what was wrong, she explained that life was just sad because everyone dies.

The death of God may have been somewhat overhyped since Nietzsche first broke the story, like those "trends" that are only occurring among about six hundred hipsters in Bushwick. It's a revolution that took place pretty much exclusively among the intelligentsia, who, now as ever, represent a negligible minority. There are no atheists in shitholes, and religion still thrives in the impoverished parts of the planet, which are, as ever, most of it. It may just be that atheists can finally come out of the closet, since this is also the first time in the last couple of millennia that atheism hasn't carried fairly severe penalties, like being hung in cages on the spires of cathedrals. (And for atheists, remember, there's no plus side to martyrdom.) Faith is a consensual, communal enterprise, and, as totalitarian states will tell you, any defection represents a threat. If only a few people believe in a religion, it's a cult; if only one person believes it, it's a delusion. Former children may remember how annoying it is when you're pretending something and some wet blanket refuses to play along, ruining it for everyone.

But as far as we know, this is the first time that any significant percentage of the human race has been atheist or agnostic. It may be too soon to say how this experiment is going, but I think even atheists would have to admit it's been something of a mixed bag. What people have chosen to worship in lieu of God is, literally, pretty dispiriting. Marx* famously called religion the opiate of the masses, but these days opiates are the opiate of the masses. I would also include things like sportfucking, shopaholism, and a constant IV feed of entertainment under the heading of mass self-medication. I sometimes wonder whether the obsession with celebrity, exhibitionism, and exhaustive self-documentation on social media isn't some sort of hysterical compensation for the absence of that omniscient Eye that used to watch and judge us. Even if your god is some capricious, abusive father—issuing arbitrary commands, demanding grotesque demonstrations of obedience, forever threatening to take off the Belt—it's still better than being an orphan.

I'd say most of my atheist friends and I are doing about as well as anyone else, limping gamely through the days with the frail defenses of kindness and laughter, books and music, late-night talks with friends and the occasional cocktail. And we seem to be at least as decent and generous-hearted as our religious peers. My friend Margot, a hard-line atheist, is one of the truest practicing Christians I know: she took a family of Laotian refugees into her home for years, flew their son back from Laos twice, and helped their oldest daughter get into an American college. Ad hoc and unglamorous though it all looks, it's actually an experiment unprecedented in history: trying to get through a human existence without delusions of either God or eternity.

When you're in the midst of a great intellectual revolution, it feels like a breakthrough, a revelation; it's easy to forget that it's another passing fashion. This last century could just be some historic aberration, a brief interim when Western civilization is temporarily adrift

* Karl, not Groucho.

between myths. The story we've used to make sense of the world for the last twenty centuries doesn't work anymore, and we haven't come up with a new one yet. The tribal shepherd god of the Old Testament, who separated land from sea and day from night six thousand years ago, seems paltry and dwarfish in the light of an observable universe ninety-three billion light-years wide, strewn with hundreds of billions of galaxies, each of which contains hundreds of billions of stars and who knows how many unimaginable alien Christs and Nietzsches, Bachs and Gandhis, Newtons and Buddhas—and, no doubt, innumerable Napoleons and Khans jealously defending their dust speck empires. People seem ill-equipped to deal with the reality unveiled by the Hubble and Large Hadron Collider, with dark energy and quantum foam; it's incomprehensible and counterintuitive, not just indifferent but utterly unrelated to human wants or fears.

Everybody smart seems to think we're in for another bad century, for wars and earthquakes and upheavals that even the creepily prescient Nietzsche couldn't have imagined: catastrophic storms and rising oceans, the depletion of the planet's resources, mass migrations and savage wars of survival. (Of all the crimes with which the Abrahamic religions could fairly be charged—and the rap sheet is a long one—the most destructive may prove to have been their promise that the world was made for us.) Nietzsche's earthquake metaphor had historical resonance: the Lisbon earthquake of 1755, which killed a hundred thousand people, triggered an intellectual referendum on theodicy after the Church offered the same lame Deuteronomic explanation that Job's sanctimonious asshole friends gave him when he was sitting on an ash-heap covered with boils: "You must've done something to deserve this." Giving obsolete, irrelevant answers to urgent new questions is lethal to an institution. Christianity has been let's say slow to respond to recent developments like the Enlightenment, the abolition of slavery and empire, and the expansion of our definitions of humanity. The Vatican formally acknowledged that Galileo had been technically correct in the matter of the heliocentric model of the solar system, after a lengthy inquiry by a committee, in 1992, the same year that radio astronomers confirmed the discovery of extrasolar planets.

Efforts to revive dead religions like Native American traditions, Druidism, and Asatru are, with all due reverence to the Æsir, moribund outside the cultural environments in which they were born. But it might be significant, a hint of things to come, that a lot of these retrofitted New Age religions share in common some variety of animism (which neuroscientists and philosophers of mind prefer to call panpsychism, so as not to sound woo-woo). The advantage of myths and religions that hold the world itself sacred are pretty evident in light of a recent UN report on the catastrophic implications of global warming: they enable us to see the world as alive, something of which we're a small, organic part, instead of as a thing we own. The current pope has issued an encyclical that repudiates consumerism and exploitation in favor of a faith that sounds suspiciously mystical: "If we feel intimately united with all that exists, then sobriety and care will well up spontaneously."

Or maybe there is no next myth. Maybe Western civilization is just out of ideas. A culture and an intellectual tradition that endured for millennia has disappeared as abruptly as dance cards and men's hats. A couple of generations ago even uneducated people knew Nimrod and Babylon, the seven virgins and the Prodigal Son; today pretty much no one's heard of any movie that was made before they were born. At least Eliot's waste land was littered with shards of Sophocles, Chaucer, and Conrad; we're a people without a culture, except for whatever we can salvage from the vast crapscape of pop songs, kids' movies, sound bites, and memes that now constitute our noosphere, like the survivors of some disaster scavenging the shambles for food and medicine and finding only Wacky Packs and Band-Aids.

Or maybe this is just my twentieth-century pessimism talking. Perhaps these present spasms aren't death throes but only the growing pains of a civilization in its adolescence. It seems like too much to hope that we might finally be ready to put aside the ancient fairy tales. Christian Fundamentalists, normally so cheered by the prospect of apocalypse, have been oddly resistant to scientists' warnings about actual imminent threats to the species, I suspect because it challenges their childlike faith that God is on top of things. The fate of the race may depend on how well we all adjust to that disillusionment that marks childhood's end: the realization that no one is going to take care of us, that we're going to have to do it all by ourselves. That we're on our own.

Diana and I broke up for the usual mundane reasons, not over matters of faith. "Don't worry about me, Tim," she told me during our breakup talk. "I believe in God." Three years later we've become close friends, more like a couple than a lot of people who are sleeping together. We finally got around to having the Jesus Conversation over a year after we'd broken up. She impressed upon me that this isn't an incidental difference between us; she really does believe in God. It's not a metaphor; the Resurrection is the central narrative—"a kind of lens," she says—through which she understands this life. What we agree on is that the question of whether life means anything is a crucial one, one we both struggle with. Because I, unlike Diana, don't have any sustaining faith, I can't always convince myself that it does, that it's inherently any better to be a bodhisattva than a junkie. But it seems telling that when I can't believe this, I start to die: I crumple into depression, addiction, potato chips and the Internet. Someone who's depressed can construct an unassailable case for self-destruction, or for humanity's deserved extinction. There's nothing intellectually invalid about nihilism; it's just incompatible with human life.

Nietzsche valued "truths" less for their empirical accuracy than for whether or not they sustained and promoted life. His own preferred truth was the Eternal Recurrence—the idea that, given an eternal universe with a finite number of particles endlessly recombining, everything that had ever happened would eventually happen all over again an infinite number of times. For him this was a kind of thought experiment, a test of what he called *amor fati* (love of one's fate), the highest imaginable affirmation of this life and the world as it is. My friend Lauren (who grew up atheist) and I have a running feud over open versus closed cosmological models. She doesn't mind the idea that the universe might continue expanding eternally and eventually gutter out in heat death. She not only doesn't mind it but perversely rejoices in it—partly, I believe, because she knows it gives me the eschatological creeps. I'm still clinging to the oscillating universe model—a sort of revised Eternal Recurrence whereby the universe will someday reach a limit to its expansion and fall back in on itself again, all of us ending up back together where it all started in a big cozy reunion, and then everything beginning all over again, like at the end of the Narnia books. Maybe I just don't like the idea of ending up alone.

It's not looking good for the oscillating model; it looks, instead, as if the universe, like us, has a finite, one-time-only life span, and eventually it'll all gutter out into absolute cold and darkness. My friend Margot, a science reporter, just did a story about the fate of the universe, describing how everything would get farther and farther apart until every elementary particle in the universe is isolated from every other. "It all sounds bleak," she concluded. The more evidence confirms this theory, the more Lauren gloats. The last time I was over at Lauren's house, her six-year-old daughter casually mentioned that she didn't believe in God, and I had to suppress a seditious impulse to lean over and whisper: "No, no, Lulu—God loves you."

I still call myself as an atheist, as opposed to an agnostic, because I hate hedging my bets and it'd only give proselytizers a chink to try to pry open with their crude crowbar arguments. Margot used to say that we had as much chance of ever imagining the true nature of God as her own goldfish did of ever understanding who she, Margot, was based on the warped, shifting shapes visible outside the fishbowl and the daily rain of manna flakes from heaven. We still don't know—it may be ontologically impossible to know—why the universe is here instead of not, why it's so improbably hospitable, or why it should be intelligible to us. We don't understand what consciousness is or how it can arise from the operations of matter. The profoundest, most insoluble problem known to us—what scientists call the Hard Problem—is how what's going on in your head at this instant can be happening at all. The more you learn about these questions, the more mysterious this world, and we in it, start to seem. This may sound similar to a religious sense, but the intellectual humility that grows out of education is very different from the complacency that arises out of ignorance. To the virtue of certitude I would oppose the idle vice of wonder. The savor of not knowing. A theology, like Diana's, of uncertainty. First thing every morning, before looking at the headlines or checking my mail, I look at a website called Astronomy Picture of the Day: stellar nurseries and supernovas, Jovian aurorae, backlit geysers on Enceladus, spiral galaxies colliding. Diana calls it "a daily practice, something akin to prayer."

I suppose you might attribute this softening of my formerly hard line on atheism—which I like to think of as a more mature, qualified philosophical stance—as so much panicky revisionism as my mortality starts to seem less abstract. Poor Nietzsche suffered the ghastliest fate imaginable, the kind of grotesquely undeserved punishment he would've recognized from Greek tragedy: reduced to a catatonic husk by some undiagnosed dementia for the last decade of his life, remanded to the care of his unscrupulous sister, who exhibited his breathing corpse to intellectual tourists and allowed his philosophy to be appropriated by proto-Nazis while his mind rotted, imprisoned in his skull. If he could have foreseen all this somehow, I don't know if even he still could have written, as he did in the prelude to *Ecce Homo*: "How could I fail to be grateful to my whole life?"

Me, I'm just hoping that I'll somehow acquire more spiritual wisdom than I now possess sometime before I die—that, after the current earthquakes and upheavals have subsided, I'll find my way to a new plateau. So far I'm not making much progress; I'm not practicing meditation or reading any sacred texts or even giving to the March of Dimes. I'm afraid I'll probably always be about like I am now: struggling feebly awhile, then giving up, struggling and giving up again, over and over, like a trapped bug. Maybe I'll go the old deathbed conversion route just to play it safe, repenting of my sins and accepting Jesus Christ as my Personal Lord and Savior right after fucking a candy striper and finally trying heroin.

Diana never felt it was her job to help people to be better, but to tell them they were fine the way they were. Most of us limp around feeling broken or defective, as if we're missing some crucial piece of human equipment. The nicest thing Diana ever said to me—one of those things I secretly inscribed in glue and glitter and hung up with yarn in my heart—was, "You seem very whole to me." She always seemed to think I was a better person than I did. I never knew whether she was deluding herself, and her affection was only for a bowdlerized version of me, or whether she saw me more clearly than I could. She pointed out to me recently that one reason she seemed so happy when we were first dating was because she was with me. How it could make Diana happy to be around me was mysterious to me, since I was always around me and I was never happy. We always forget the Heisenberg effect of our own presence—that we only ever get to see what other people are like when we're around. I'd been drawn to her hoping I might absorb some of her radiance, not realizing it was, in part, my own reflected light.

I Never Went to Iceland

I suppose I should say I *didn't* go to Iceland—*never* sounds a little melodramatic. It's not as if I've died and all hope of ever having gone to Iceland is obviated. But for some reason this missed opportunity is occasioning more than the usual level of regret. I've had a free apartment in Reykjavík to stay in on offer for several years, and somehow I've never made it there. The owner sends me photos of the aurora borealis that look as hopelessly distant to me as Hubble photos of stellar nebulae.

This was going to be the summer I finally went. Airfares were cheap. I'd just finished writing a draft of a manuscript in May, and for the first time in three years the awful obligation to Work on My Book was not weighing on my soul. The summer looked as wide-open and shimmering with possibility as the summer vacations of childhood.

But events conspired against me. I just couldn't afford the flight until a check I was waiting on arrived, and although all other transactions in the twenty-first century are conducted electronically and instantaneously, writers are still paid through a system of scriveners, countinghouses, and small boys dispatched on errands with shillings in their pockets. So by the time I had enough money, I'd run out of summer.

Other unexpected complications arose, like they always do. I'd also intended to be less of recluse this summer, to see old friends more often, make regular trips down to Baltimore and have visitors at my cabin every weekend. But just before the Fourth of July, a visiting friend nearly tore off her little toe falling down the stairs at my house, and was laid up on crutches at my place for the next several weeks. She tried to be as independent as possible, but there are limits to what a woman with two surgical pins in her toe can do, so my job became to fetch objects for her, make her tea, and occasionally convey her from place to place, carrying her like the Creature from the Black Lagoon abducting his beloved, the girl in the white one-piece.

She'd recovered enough to go home by the end of July, and since then I've been frantically cramming all the idle goofing off I didn't get to do all summer into its last few weeks. But goofing off isn't the sort of thing you can cram. Now every reminder of time squandered—the empty hammock I hardly ever lay in, a little sugar cube melon that went bad before I'd cut even one slice from it—makes me want to cry. (Is there a word, perhaps in French, for nostalgia for the present? One Japanese scholar coined the term *mono no aware*—an exquisite, wistful sensitivity to the ephemerality of all things.) This end-of-summer melancholy is commonplace, as endemic to August as chest colds are to February. Part of it is just my hatred and dread of back-to-school time, unchanged since childhood. The whole world of work and productivity still seems to me like an unconscionable waste of time; the only parts of life that we'll remember with any joy are the summers, the Saturdays, the smoke breaks and happy hours, the stolen in-between moments and goofing off.

But there's something else lurking underneath this moping, something scarier. I use the word *never* in my Icelandic lament because there is attached to it a sense of desolation, as of a possibility lost forever. For me, at least, it feels less like melancholy, which is a gentle, almost pleasant emotion, than suppressed terror. It's only the superficial throb of a pain that goes much deeper, in the same the way that these few oddly cool days in August are the first innocuous evidence of an entire planet tilting inexorably into the shadow.

I'm not old but I'm not young anymore, either, and if you're a daydreamer and a ditherer like me, you can manage to sustain until well into midlife the delusion that you might yet get around to doing all the things you meant to do: making a movie, getting married, living in Paris. But at some point you start to suspect that you might not end up doing that stuff after all, and have to consider the possibility that the life you have right now might be pretty much it: your life. This realization could, in theory, free you to experience your actual life instead of dismissing it as an unimportant prelude to the good part, or comparing it to the imaginary one you plotted out for yourself at age twelve, or back in May. The spring romance I'd hoped might turn into a lasting relationship culminated, instead, in a really unpleasant overnight visit. But I found myself involved instead with someone made sanguine by tragedy, with the alien capacity to appreciate whatever happiness comes her way without either second-guessing it to death or crushing it by grasping at it clamoring for more. She's a hypnotherapist, and I've been thinking of asking her whether it'd be possible to induce a similar quality in me.

Because although I didn't go to Iceland this summer, I did take care of a friend. The time she and I spent together, conscripted into our roles as invalid and manservant, was kind of like going on a cross-country road trip or to sleepaway camp together. We're now less like friends than siblings or an old married couple: we have running in-jokes and recurring squabbles and speak a language of catchphrases incomprehensible to outsiders ("You got to put it *on the Moose*!"). We call ourselves Heroes of Fun. We may briefly hate each other now and then but we're doomed to love each other forever. Once you've carried someone in your arms while she's bleeding, you are never indifferent to her again.

I didn't go to Iceland, but I ate Taco Bell while watching *Zapped!* in a hospital bed late at night, spent indolent afternoons drinking wine on a back porch garlanded with honeysuckle in Baltimore, played a little cornhole at a pleasure club (not what it sounds like), and opened a humane mousetrap only to have the captive mouse spring out straight into my face while a friend was trying to leave an "out-of-office" voice mail message, which suddenly erupted into a chaos of little-girl screams and berserk cursing. I swam naked in the Chesapeake Bay, made martinis at five every day, and watched fireflies after dark. I learned, late in life, that I am competent in a crisis, and a good dancer. I lay in a field spotting satellites with my ex-girlfriend Margot and saw a Perseid meteor streak across the sky. It vanished so fast it was hard to tell whether its incandescent trail was in the atmosphere, on my retina, or only in memory.

I suspect that the way I feel now, at summer's end, is about how I'll feel at the end of my life, assuming I have time and mind enough left to reflect: bewildered by how unexpectedly everything turned out, regretful about all the things I didn't get around to, clutching the handful of friends and funny stories I've amassed, and wondering where it all went. And I'll probably still be evading the same fact I'm evading now: that the life I ended up with, much as I complain about it, was pretty much the one I wanted. And that whatever dissatisfactions I have with it are really with my own character.

In a couple of weeks I'll resume teaching for the fall, and start boarding up my psyche for another hateful winter in New York. But the summer's unconsummated lust for travel still torments me. A couple of weeks ago I went to the American Museum of Natural History and it occurred to me, looking at the dioramas in the Hall of North American Mammals, that I would come to this museum to look at those dioramas even without any animals in them. It's like a peep show of nature for New Yorkers. Those realistic vistas of Alaskan glaciers, the Great Plains, and Yosemite National Park pull at my insides with a longing that hurts. God, how I long to go out west again someday—to drive some blue highway in Nevada or Utah until there's absolutely nothing around me, then stop the car, in the middle of the road, maybe, and get out and just stand there, where I can see from one horizon to the other, and smell the air and feel the sun and listen to the silence of the desert. I have this idea that if I could do this, time might hold still for a second, and I would know, for just a moment, what it feels like to be here.

Acknowledgments

The people who always believed in this book and got me through the writing of it were: Amber Qureshi, my editor-for-life; Emily Scott, friend and spiritual advisor; and my agent, the feared Meg Thompson—cheerleader, bodyguard, blue fairy. And, of course, the Friend of the Man, poet James Boyd White.

Jon Karp, president and publisher of Simon & Schuster, gave me as much time as I needed to write this book, which turned out to be a lot. This book had two editors at Simon & Schuster, Jon Cox and Sean Manning: Jon saw this book drunk with its pants off and poured black coffee down its throat and made it halfway presentable; Sean gave it a last-minute hair smoothing and tie straightening before shoving it out onstage. Copyeditor David Chesanow spared me many an embarrassment and unearthed even grislier details of the New Fire ceremony. Thanks also to the editors who refined earlier versions of some of these essays: Peter Catapano of the *New York Times*, whom I would trust to edit my work sight unseen; Mark Healy of *Men's Journal*; and Molly Pisani (née Lindley), formerly of Simon & Schuster.

Thanks to my other, unpaid readers—Myla Goldberg, Nell Greenfieldboyce, Martha Joseph, Megan Kelso, Laura Kipnis, Dana Jeri Maier, and Ellen Twaddell. And to all my other advisors, collaborators, conversationalists, and benefactors: Chris Beck, Jenny Boylan, Claire and Emma Connolly, Dave Dudley, Carolyn Ewald, Jim Fisher, Lisa Hanawalt, Tom Hart, Sam Holden, Isabelle Johnson, Mildred Kreider, Aaron Long, Sadie Lune, Steve McLoughlin, Alex Robinson, Melissa Shaw, Mishka Shubaly, the (Formerly?) Evil Ben Walker, Robin Wetherill, and the Peripatetic Wednesday crowd. And thanks sincerely to everyone who consented to be written about.

Thanks to Brian Morton for proofing "Orientation" against professional ruin, and to Meghan Jablonski, PhD, for reading "The Strange Situation" for accuracy. "The Strange Situation" grew out of a talk I gave to the Phi Alpha Society at NYU, to which I was invited by Jessica Leif; "The Uncertainty Principle" came out of a talk I gave at the Mockingbird Conference, to which I was invited by David Zahl. Thanks to them for the inspiration.

The writing of such a book requires a support team of mental and physical health professionals. I am indebted to Libby Kessman, Drs. Kristina Eipl and Katherine Fichtel, Liat Forti, and Donna Vida for morale restoration and maintenance.

Special thanks to Dr. Silvia Bell for the interview, and for an enjoyable game.

Deepest gratitude, highest hopes, and purest love to my first creative nonfiction writing class, fall semester of 2014.

O my beloved cat!